Child and Adolescent Clinical Psychopharmacology Made Simple

second edition

JOHN D. PRESTON, PSY.D., ABPP
JOHN H. O'NEAL, MD
MARY C. TALAGA, R.PH., PH.D.

New Harbinger Publications, Inc.

Publisher's Note

This publication is designed to provide accurate and authoritative information in regard to the subject matter covered. It is sold with the understanding that the publisher is not engaged in rendering psychological, financial, legal, or other professional services. If expert assistance or counseling is needed, the services of a competent professional should be sought.

Distributed in Canada by Raincoast Books

Copyright © 2010 by John Preston, John H. O'Neal, & Mary C. Talaga
New Harbinger Publications, Inc.
5674 Shattuck Avenue
Oakland, CA 94609
www.newharbinger.com

Acquired by Catharine Sutker; Cover design by Amy Shoup;
Edited by Kayla Sussell; Text design by Tracy Marie Carlson

Library of Congress Cataloging-in-Publication Data

Preston, John, 1950-
   Child and adolescent clinical psychopharmacology made simple / John Preston, John H. O'Neal, and Mary C. Talaga. -- 2nd ed.
      p. ; cm.
   Includes bibliographical references and index.
   ISBN-13: 978-1-57224-703-1 (pbk. : alk. paper)
   ISBN-10: 1-57224-703-7 (pbk. : alk. paper)   1. Pediatric psychopharmacology. 2. Adolescent psychopharmacology. I. O'Neal, John H. II. Talaga, Mary C. III. Title.
   [DNLM: 1. Mental Disorders--drug therapy. 2. Adolescent. 3. Child. 4. Psychotropic Drugs--therapeutic use. WS 350 P938c 2009]
   RJ504.7.P74 2009
   618.92'89061--dc22

FSC
Mixed Sources
Product group from well-managed forests and other controlled sources
Cert no. SW-COC-002283
www.fsc.org
© 1996 Forest Stewardship Council

12 11 10

10 9 8 7 6 5 4 3 2 1   First printing

To Dr. Bill Bergquist, friend and mentor

—JP

In memory of Patrick Everette Cummings....
Your spirit lives on.

—MT

To my patients, for they have been my best teachers.

—JO

Contents

Acknowledgments

Many thanks to our publisher, Dr. Matthew McKay, and our most excellent editors, Catharine Sutker, Karen Stein, and Kayla Sussell.

Thanks to our families, with deep appreciation for their patience and encouragement.

Finally, a heartfelt thanks to our patients.
May this book help our fellow mental health clinicians in our shared and ongoing struggle to reduce emotional suffering in young people.

INTRODUCTION

Sharing Our Concerns: For Health Care Providers, Parents, and Patients

Facts without values, fragmentary specialties with no integrating philosophy of life as a whole, data with no ethical standards for their use, techniques ... with no convictions about life's ultimate meaning ... here a panacea has turned out to be a problem.

—Harry Emerson Fosdick
The Living of These Days (1956)

Many young people experience considerable emotional suffering. Oftentimes this psychological pain is associated with poverty, poor prenatal care, racial or other forms of discrimination, serious family dysfunction, traumatic life events, or any of a host of neuropsychiatric disorders. Only certain types of emotional distress are appropriate for treatment with psychiatric medications.

Psychiatric medication treatment of children and teenagers began in the 1960s. Yet only recently have large-scale medication trials been conducted. The research in child psychiatry is still considered to be limited. Clearly advances have been made, both in the safety of medications and in the development of treatment guidelines. In this book we summarize basic information regarding classes of psychological disorders for which medications are often prescribed, and we present current guidelines for the use of medications. However, we first want to state three important and overarching concerns.

The first concern is that in the current era of managed care, it is common for insufficient time or attention to be given to conducting a comprehensive history and diagnostic evaluation. Such an evaluation is essential before any recommendation can be made regarding treatment. Second, it is clear that when psychiatric medications are used to treat particular disorders, close follow-up is warranted and essential for addressing problems of treatment adherence, managing side effects, and monitoring response to treatment. Third, most children and teenagers suffering from psychological problems do not require medication treatment; instead, they may need to receive psychosocial interventions, often involving the family as well as the individual. Even in those conditions that are judged to be largely neurobiological in nature and responsive to medication treatments, psychotherapy is *always* indicated.

Our voicing these three issues may seem as if we are just stating the obvious; however, our concern is that with the quick-fix and get-on-with-your-life mentality in our social culture and the health care industry's focus on cost containment, the knee-jerk reaction of too many providers may be to reach for the prescription pad whenever they see psychological symptoms. While the appropriate use of psychiatric medications has helped many young people, it is so important for us to strongly endorse a comprehensive approach to treatment. This approach should be based on careful evaluations, close monitoring, and the use of psychotherapy, with medications prescribed only if warranted.

It is also important for clinicians and consumers alike to be aware of the risks and benefits of all treatments. Because of the enormous complexity of human psychological functioning, most problems are multidimensional and require interventions on a number of levels. And it is equally important to be humble regarding our approaches to treatment. Psychiatric drugs, as we shall see in this volume, can reduce rates of suicide, may decrease the risk of substance abuse, and in some instances may prevent certain kinds of brain damage. But medical treatments also have clear limits; there are no panaceas. No drug can mend a broken heart, fill an empty life, or teach parents how to love their children.

CHAPTER 1

Issues in Psychopharmacological Treatment of Children and Adolescents

In this first chapter we address a number of general issues that are important to consider prior to discussing diagnosis and treatment, which we'll cover in the chapters that follow.

DIAGNOSING AND TREATING CHILDREN AND ADOLESCENTS

Until just recently, in child psychiatry there appeared to be an assumption that children with psychiatric disorders were quite similar, if not identical, to adults with respect to both diagnostic and pharmacological treatment issues. The recommended approach was to diagnose and treat as you would with adults, although generally starting treatment with lower doses of medications. Even though there is some degree of symptomatic overlap between adult- and childhood-onset disorders, there are also significant features that distinguish psychiatric syndromes as well as pharmacological treatments in children and adults. It must also be kept in mind that the target of psychiatric drugs (the central nervous system) is continuously undergoing maturational changes throughout childhood and adolescence. Certain neurotransmitter systems are not fully online in children, and some brain structures have not reached full development. In a sense, using psychotropic drugs with younger clients is like shooting at a moving target. Likewise, there are significant differences between adults and younger people in the way the drugs are metabolized. Kids are not just smaller versions of adults.

It is likely that the majority of emotional suffering experienced by youngsters is related to situational stress and responds best to nonmedical, psychological treatments (e.g., family therapy). However, it is also becoming increasingly clear that many major mental illnesses begin in childhood (for example, 33 percent of obsessive-compulsive disorder cases and up to 25 percent of bipolar disorder cases have childhood or early-adolescent onset). Not only do these disorders cause considerable suffering in young children, but they can also markedly interfere with normal social and academic developmental experiences. For example, more than one-half of children experiencing major depression continue to be symptomatic for more than 2 years. During depressive episodes, many experience significant social withdrawal and academic failure, often due to an impaired ability to concentrate. Even if they recover, many of these children find it hard to ever catch up academically or socially.

Increasing evidence also shows that some psychiatric disorders are subject to progressive neurobiological impairment if they go untreated (the kindling model of disease progression). Toxic levels of neurotransmitters, such as glutamate, or stress hormones, such as cortisol, may damage neural tissue or interfere with normal patterns of neuromaturation (see figure 1-A). Pharmacological treatment of these disorders may be not only successful in improving symptoms but also neuroprotective (in other words, medication treatment may either protect against brain damage or promote normal neuromaturation; in some instances, medications may promote the regeneration of nerve cells, a process called *neurogenesis*).

DISORDERS WITH EVIDENCE OF PROGRESSIVE NEUROBIOLOGICAL IMPAIRMENT

- Bipolar illness

- Attention-deficit/hyperactivity disorder (ADHD)

- Schizophrenia

- Some cases of recurrent unipolar depression

- Some cases of post-traumatic stress disorder

Figure 1-A

INFORMED CONSENT AND ADDRESSING PARENTAL CONCERNS

In addition to clinical considerations, other unique challenges arise in the prescribing of psychotropic medications for children. Children cannot give true *informed consent* since parents are the ones who usually decide whether or not to allow medication treatment. This presents at least four concerns: (1) fears about drug use (or possible addiction) may lead parents to withhold treatment from some children who need it; (2) some parents may see psychiatric disorders simply as chemical imbalances, believe that pills will fix the problem, and ignore psychological factors (such as dysfunctional family dynamics) as a focus for treatment; (3) parents may use medications primarily for behavioral control despite detrimental side effects (for example, excessive doses of stimulants may markedly reduce hyperactive behavior in children with attention-deficit/hyperactivity disorder, even causing lethargy and sedation and, if doses become too high, decreased cognitive functioning); and (4) the young person is left out of the loop, perhaps not consulted about how he or she feels about medication treatment.

Most pediatric clinicians agree that children should be included in discussions about psychiatric medication treatment (especially for children ages seven and older whose cognitive development has proceeded enough that they can understand some information regarding medication treatment). Providing information is important in order to encourage the child to voice concerns about treatment, since many children conclude that if they need medicine, they must be very ill or "crazy." Also, these early experiences with psychiatric treatment, if perceived to be beneficial by the child, may go a long way toward instilling positive attitudes about mental health treatment (this is a critical point, since many of the more severe disorders that warrant medical treatment during childhood are the first manifestations of what may be lifelong mental illnesses). Including the child in discussions regarding medication treatment can often give him or her a feeling of respect and thereby foster a positive relationship with the therapist or physician.

Because parents who do not wholeheartedly endorse treatment will often sabotage it, professionals need to devote a good deal of time to addressing all of their concerns about drug treatment. Informed consent should also include the risks of not treating certain disorders.

Parental Fears Regarding Drug Addiction

Many parents are understandably concerned about the use of habit-forming drugs to treat their children. It is important to talk openly with parents about these concerns (even if they do not initiate the conversation). Among psychiatric medications, only two classes encompass potential drugs of abuse: stimulants (such as Ritalin) and benzodiazepines (antianxiety drugs such as Xanax). However, the vast majority of children with psychiatric disorders do not abuse these medications. Although stimulants can be abused by those genetically predisposed toward substance abuse, such drugs generally do not produce euphoria in ADHD children. In fact, many children with ADHD experience mild dysphoric effects from stimulants. Additionally, current data strongly indicates that among those with ADHD, the use of stimulants actually decreases the risk of substance abuse by about 50 percent in comparison to drug abuse rates among nontreated ADHD subjects (Biederman, et al., 1999; Kuczenski & Segal, 2002; Mannuzza, Klein, & Moulton, 2003).

Substance abuse by children and adolescents is a common and serious concern in our society. It must also be kept in mind that untreated mental illnesses result in significant emotional suffering and contribute to a much higher likelihood of drug abuse down the line. Low self-esteem, depression, anxiety, and a sense of alienation often prompt the use of illicit drugs as a form of self-medication. Thus any risk-benefit assessment of medication treatment and drug abuse must certainly take into consideration the risks of failure to treat the psychiatric disorder.

MEDICATIONS AND THE MEDIA

Research studies and clinical experience certainly influence prescribing practices. However, in recent years the media has had a profound effect on public opinion and ultimately on clinical practice. Public opinions are often influenced by both drug companies' marketing efforts (and thus their profit motives) and news headlines, an example of which is the recent concern over antidepressant use in children and its possible relationship with increased suicidality, an issue discussed in more detail in chapter 2.

In the late 1980s negative attention was focused on the drug Ritalin, a widely prescribed stimulant used to treat ADHD. Andrew Brotman (1992), summarizing the work of Safer and Krager (1992), states, "The media attack was led by major national television talk show hosts and in the opinion of the authors, allowed anecdotal and unsubstantiated allegations concerning Ritalin to be aired. There were also over twenty lawsuits initiated throughout the country, most by a lawyer linked to the Church of Scientology."

In a study conducted in Baltimore, Maryland, examining the effects of this negative media and litigation blitz, Safer and Krager found that during the 2-year period just following the negative media attention, prescriptions for Ritalin had dropped by 40 percent. What were the consequences? Of those children who discontinued use of Ritalin, 36 percent experienced major academic maladjustment (such as failing grades or suspension) and another 47 percent had mild to moderate academic problems. During this time there was a 400 percent increase in the prescription of tricyclic antidepressants (TCA), which were then being used in place of Ritalin (studies had demonstrated that tricyclics were somewhat effective in treating ADHD symptoms but clearly much less effective than stimulants). Further, tricyclics are considerably more toxic, have much higher rates of side effects, and have been associated with sudden cardiac-related deaths in six children. Clearly, parents had heard the negative reports about Ritalin in the media and approached their pediatricians with concerns about the drug. As a result, many children were taken off the stimulant and put on a class of drugs that are less effective and considerably more dangerous.

Media attention is important in that it can alert consumers and professionals (including the Food and Drug Administration [FDA]) to possible problems with certain medications. When this leads to more thorough investigations, sometimes drugs are found to be problematic or unsafe. However, it can also lead to unwarranted fears and ultimately to clinical decisions that may not be in the best interest of our clients. The point is that media-driven concerns raised by our clients and their parents can be significant, and we as clinicians must be aware of and sensitive to such concerns.

DRUG RESEARCH AND OUTCOME STUDIES

As important as efficacy studies are, there is a relative paucity of good studies in child psychopharmacology (with the notable exception of the numerous well-controlled studies of the treatment of ADHD with stimulants). In the past, pharmaceutical companies did not conduct tests of psychiatric drugs on children. However, in 1998 the Food and Drug Administration mandated that safety studies be carried out for new psychiatric drugs with child subjects, and has recently begun offering financial incentives (in the form of extensions of patents) for conducting efficacy studies with children. Thus, in very recent times, better-controlled studies have been initiated, although many of these are not yet published and some suffer from significant methodological flaws. It is hoped that in the next few years the number of well-done studies will increase significantly.

Another concern is that many studies do not include severely ill children (the reason being that it is not considered ethical to expose severely disturbed children to placebos over a period of months). Thus, in some child psychiatry studies involving random assignment and the use of placebos, groups of subjects often include only mild to moderately severe cases. Information about treatment outcomes for severely ill kids is often limited to that which comes from clinical experience and case studies. It is important to keep these research limitations in mind when evaluating the outcomes of medication studies.

A third area of concern, both for clinicians and parents, is the effect of very long-term use of psychiatric medications in children. Short-term side effects are well documented and will be discussed in detail in subsequent chapters. However, there is relatively little hard data that indicates the risks associated with long-term treatments. Yet, for many of the disorders discussed in this book, including bipolar disorder, ADHD, and psychotic disorders, long-term medication treatment is strongly recommended. It is our belief that when this topic arises in discussions with patients and their parents, the clinician's only appropriate response is to be completely candid about the lack of knowledge regarding long-term drug exposure, but to also be clear about the risks of not treating certain disorders. Deciding whether to use medication is always a matter of evaluating risk versus benefit, and parents need to be offered as much information as possible so they can make informed choices.

MEDICATION METABOLISM IN YOUNG CLIENTS

The normal rate of hepatic (liver) metabolism is high in children until the time of puberty. The result is that most medications are aggressively metabolized in the liver and rapidly excreted. Because what ultimately matters is how much of the drug enters the bloodstream, treatment of prepubertal children may require doses that approach or equal those for adults. (The use of seemingly high doses for young children may seem counterintuitive to many parents, and thus it will be helpful for clinicians to explain the role of increased rates of drug metabolism.)

During the 2 to 4 months surrounding the entry into puberty, the rate of hepatic metabolism significantly slows. For this reason, youngsters who have been on a maintenance dose of psychiatric medication and tolerating it well may begin to show increasing side effects when this change in metabolic rate occurs and more of the drug begins to escape the liver and enter circulation. Dosage adjustments may then be required to minimize side effects.

APPROVED DRUGS AND OFF-LABEL USE

Currently very few psychiatric drugs are approved by the FDA for use in treating children and young adolescents. Yet these drugs are also in widespread use in child psychiatry. It is very common practice in the field, and in general medicine, to prescribe drugs *off label,* meaning the use of drugs that are approved by the FDA for treatment of certain conditions but are being used to treat other conditions. For example, the anticonvulsant medication Tegretol (carbamazepine) is FDA approved for the treatment of epilepsy but not bipolar disorder. However, Tegretol has been used for a number of years to treat some cases of mania. Since clinical and scientific research supports the use of this drug in treating mania, its use is considered to be in keeping with medical standards of practice, and thus neither illegal nor unethical. Likewise, many drugs approved for use in adults (but not in children) are used to treat child psychiatric patients. For example, only one antidepressant (fluoxetine, or Prozac) has been approved by the FDA for the treatment of major depression in children, yet many other antidepressants are used to treat childhood-onset depression.

Some drug classes, most notably antidepressants, have been found effective in treating a host of disorders other than depression, such as panic disorder, OCD, social anxiety, and so on. We will discuss the use of antidepressants in more detail in chapter 2, and in later chapters we will address how such drugs play a role in the treatment of other disorders.

ATTITUDES AND REALITIES REGARDING PSYCHOPHARMACOLOGY WITH CHILDREN AND ADOLESCENTS

Despite the fact that some of the disorders discussed in the following chapters are deemed to be due largely to a primary neurobiological cause and require drug treatment, we categorically state, as we did in the introduction, that no child should ever be treated with psychiatric medications without concurrent psychotherapy. It is common for pediatricians to diagnose and prescribe psychotropic medications, and in very rare cases pediatricians have both appropriate training for diagnosing and treating psychiatric disorders and enough time to conduct a comprehensive evaluation. Yet the reality is that most primary care doctors are overwhelmed with patients and have grossly inadequate amounts of time to devote to taking careful histories and conducting thorough diagnostic evaluations. We strongly believe that children with serious mental illnesses should be evaluated and treated by mental health specialists.

WHERE WE GO FROM HERE

In the chapters that follow we will discuss specific classes of psychiatric disorders. The initial focus of each chapter will be on important issues regarding diagnosis, highlighting new developments in the diagnosis of childhood disorders. This will be followed by an overview of medications that are commonly used to treat particular disorders, and then specific treatment guidelines. Please note that the appendix of this book includes general information sheets regarding six common classes of psychotropic drugs that may be given to patients or used by caregivers. We believe that it is very important for consumers to become knowledgeable about treatment options and the risks and benefits of medications. Please feel free to make copies of these sheets and use them as handouts in your practice.

CHAPTER 2

Depression

Accurate prevalence rates for adjustment disorders with depressed mood in children are not available, although the rates are likely to be high. However, epidemiologic studies have established that yearly prevalence rates of major depression are significant (2 percent for children and 10 percent for teenagers). Of great concern is the fact that serious depressive episodes in children and young adolescents are also likely to herald the onset of either severe and highly recurrent unipolar depression (35 percent of cases) or bipolar disorder (48 percent), based on ten-year follow-up after an index episode of depression (Geller et al., 2002; Geller & DelBello, 2003).

Central to the treatment of severe depression is not only reducing the suffering and disability experienced in the current episode but also anticipating these extraordinarily high rates of recurrence and addressing relapse prevention.

DIAGNOSTIC ISSUES

Although there are similarities between childhood-onset and adult-onset major depression, there are also notable differences. Use of the *Diagnostic and Statistical Manual of Mental Disorders* (fourth edition; *DSM-IV*) (1994) standard criteria for diagnosing major depression failed to accurately diagnose 76 percent of young children judged to be suffering with major depression (Luby et al., 2002). For more diagnostic precision, Luby et al. recommend the modified diagnostic criteria listed in figure 2-A.

SYMPTOMS OF MAJOR DEPRESSION

- Depressed or irritable mood for more days than not

Plus 4 of the following (as opposed to the 5 required for adults to be diagnosed with major depression):

- Anhedonia

- Significant weight loss or gain

- Insomnia or hypersomnia more days than not

- Psychomotor agitation or retardation

- Fatigue more days than not

- Feelings of worthlessness or excessive guilt

- Impaired concentration

- Recurrent thoughts of death or suicide

Figure 2-A

It is of interest that for many years children with major depression were not believed to have vegetative signs (such as sleep or appetite disturbance), although these symptoms do occur in 80 percent or more of youngsters with major depression. Also, it is important to note that in children with depression an irritable or anhedonic mood is much more common than a sad or depressed mood. See figure 2-B for a list of additional depressive symptoms.

ADDITIONAL DIAGNOSTIC SIGNS AND SYMPTOMS OF MAJOR DEPRESSION IN CHILDREN

Most Common Symptoms

- Irritability

- Social withdrawal

- Anhedonia

- Low self-esteem

- Themes of death, suicide, or self-destruction appearing in play

- Vegetative symptoms (such as sleep disturbance)

Common Symptoms

- School failure

- Loneliness

- Sadness

- Low energy

Associated Signs and Symptoms

- Vague, nonspecific physical complaints

- Running away from home

- Boredom

- Extreme sensitivity to rejection or failure

- Reckless behavior; acting out

- Difficulty with relationships

- Substance use or abuse

Figure 2-B

In almost half of prepubertal children with episodes of major depression, the episode ultimately turns out to have been the first manifestation of bipolar illness. Of people with prepubertal bipolar disorder, 70 percent initially present with depression and, on average, have two to four depressive episodes prior to their first manic episode (Geller & DelBello, 2003). Thus the clinician, in addition to making a diagnosis of major depression, must also conduct a comprehensive evaluation to rule out potential bipolarity in all depressed children and teenagers. This is especially critical in light of the growing concern that the use of antidepressants may, in the long run, be risky in bipolar patients (potentially exacerbating a manic episode or causing cycle acceleration, a worsening of the disorder, discussed in chapter 3). The history and clinical features given in figure 2-C should alert the clinician to a higher risk of bipolar disorder.

RED FLAGS FOR POSSIBLE BIPOLAR DISORDER

- Atypical depressive symptoms such as hypersomnia (excessive sleeping), severe fatigue, increased appetite, carbohydrate craving, and weight gain

- Seasonal (winter) depressions

- Psychotic symptoms

- History of separation anxiety disorder

- History of attention-deficit/hyperactivity disorder (ADHD) or ADHD-like symptoms*

- Positive family history of bipolar disorder

- History of hypomania

---

* Most children with a history of ADHD do not develop bipolar disorder, but some individuals with prepubertal-onset bipolar disorder do show a history of behaviors during infancy and early childhood that resemble ADHD. This topic will be addressed more extensively in chapters 3 and 6.

Figure 2-C

PSYCHOPHARMACOLOGY

Efficacy of Antidepressants

Early case reports and clinical experience have shown that *very severely depressed, hospitalized* children and adolescents often did respond to treatment with tricyclic antidepressants (Walkup, 2004). At the same time, tricyclics can have significant side effects, are very toxic in overdoses, and have been associated with six cases of sudden death in children (due to cardiac effects with the tricyclic desipramine). Additionally, in recent controlled studies tricyclics have been found to be no more effective than placebos in the treatment of mild to moderate major depression (as mentioned earlier, severely ill children are not included in such studies). Thus in this chapter we will only address the newer (nontricyclic) antidepressants.

To date, the double-blind, placebo-controlled studies of antidepressants in the treatment of major depression have been limited to selective serotonin reuptake inhibitors (SSRIs) and, in one study, venlafaxine (although drugs such as bupropion are in common use and other classes of drugs are undergoing trials). Placebo responses in these child studies are higher than those seen in adult studies; thus, in order to be judged, from a statistical standpoint, significantly better than placebo, the drug must have a very high level of demonstrated efficacy and large enough sample sizes. The limited studies in this area of investigation reveal that SSRIs are much better tolerated than tricyclics and are significantly more effective than either placebos or tricyclics (Emslie & Mayes, 2001; Wagner et al., 2003; March et al., 2004; Whittington et al., 2004).

However, a meta-analysis of studies by Jureidini et al. (2004) shows an effect size across six randomized, placebo-controlled studies of just 0.26. This is a very small effect size and *may* suggest that antidepressant efficacy is limited compared to placebo. On the other hand, it is important to note that most of the studies reviewed in this meta-analysis suffered from significant methodological flaws (Walkup, 2004). These studies were supported by pharmaceutical companies and done largely in response to an FDA incentive: "Companies could extend their patents for a drug for six months by testing it on children...whether the trial demonstrated that the drug worked or not. There was, in other words, a powerful incentive to do the trials, but no incentive to do them well" (Mahler, 2004).

A more recent, large-scale, federally funded program, Treatments for Adolescents with Depression Study (TADS), has addressed many of the methodological issues raised in other studies. The sample included 432 adolescents (ages 12 to 17) suffering from major depression. The subjects were randomly assigned to one of four groups. At the completion of the 12 weeks of treatment, the percentages of positive responders were: placebo, 35 percent; cognitive behavioral therapy (CBT), 43 percent; fluoxetine (Prozac), 61 percent; and combination CBT and fluoxetine, 71 percent. Here, drug treatments were significantly more effective than placebo or psychotherapy alone. The effect sizes were 0.8 and 0.6 for the combination treatment and fluoxetine alone, respectively (March et al., 2004; Glass, 2004). Obviously, these results are more promising and also underscore the benefits of combining medication treatment with psychotherapy.

In evaluating high placebo response rates, which are common, it is very important to keep in mind that, although acute treatment placebo responses in children are impressively high, no study has evaluated the ability of placebos to prevent breakthrough symptoms or to reduce episode recurrence. Currently available efficacy studies are limited in duration (8 to 18 weeks) and there is an absence of long-term follow-up. Typically positive placebo responses, if they occur, tend to be time limited. Owing to the highly recurrent nature of depression in youngsters, the issue of longer-term effects is crucial, although no existing systematic data address this issue.

Two findings from these empirical studies and clinical experience appear to be important to note: (1) the time to onset of positive medication effects may be longer for children than for adults (with children, although symptomatic improvement may be noted within 4 weeks, in some instances an adequate trial of 8 to 12 weeks is required), and (2) a syndrome of apathy/amotivation or emotional disinhibition, sometimes seen in adults on chronic SSRI treatment, is more commonly encountered in children (Walkup, 2004; Barnhart, Makela, & Latocha, 2004).

An Overview of Antidepressant Medications

Currently only one antidepressant, fluoxetine (Prozac, Sarafem), is approved by the FDA for the treatment of major depression in children (ages 8 and older); however, as mentioned in chapter 1, many antidepressants are in widespread off-label use. Antidepressants are commonly listed in most psychopharmacology textbooks according to the neurotransmitters they target: SSRIs (selective serotonin reuptake inhibitors), NRIs (norepinephrine reuptake inhibitors), SNRIs (serotonin and norepinephrine reuptake inhibitors), NDRIs (norepinephrine and dopamine reuptake inhibitors), and atypical antidepressants (trazodone and mirtazapine). Antidepressant medications are listed by class, names, recommended starting doses, and daily doses in figure 2-D, and common side effects are listed in figure 2-E.

ANTIDEPRESSANT MEDICATIONS				
Generic Name	**Brand Name**	**Starting Dose (mg)**	**Daily Dose (mg)**	**Daily Dose (Weight Adjusted, mg/kg^2)**
SSRI				
Fluoxetine	Prozac, Sarafem	C[1]: 5 A[1]: 10	5–40 10–60	0.25–0.75
Sertraline	Zoloft	C: 25 A: 50	25–200 50–200	1.5–3
Paroxetine	Paxil	C: 5 A: 10	10–30 20–50	0.25–0.75
Citalopram	Celexa	C: 10 A: 10	10–40 10–40	0.25–0.75
Escitalopram	Lexapro	C: 5 A: 5	5–20 5–20	0.125–0.375
Fluvoxamine	Luvox	C: 25 A: 25–50	25–200 50–200	1.5–4.5
SNRI				
Venlafaxine XR	Effexor XR	C: 12.5 A: 25–37.5	12.5–37.5 25–75+	1–2
Desvenla-faxine	Pristiq	C: not established A: 50	not established 50–300	not established
Duloxetine	Cymbalta	C: not established A: 10	not established 40–100	1
NRI				
Atomoxetine	Strattera	C: 10 A: 40	10–60 40–100	1.2–1.8

NDRI				
Bupropion SR	Wellbutrin SR	C: 100 A: 100	50–150 150–300	3–6
Atypical				
Mirtazapine	Remeron	C: 7.5 A: 15	15–30 15–45	not established
Trazodone[3]	Desyrel	C: 25 A: 50	25–75 25–100	1–3

1 C: prepubertal children; A: adolescents

2 To convert pounds to kilograms, divide number of pounds by 2.2.

3 Trazodone is technically an antidepressant but has limited efficacy in treating depression. However, it is often used as a non-habit-forming medication for the treatment of initial insomnia. The doses in the chart are those used to treat insomnia.

Figure 2-D

COMMON SIDE EFFECTS OF ANTIDEPRESSANTS

Medication	Activation[1]	Sedation	Nausea	Sexual Dysfunction[2]	Weight Gain
SSRI					
Fluoxetine	+++	+/0	+	++	3
Sertraline	++	+/0	++	++	3
Paroxetine	+	++	+	++	3
Citalopram	+	+/0	+	++	3
Escitalopram	+	+/0	+	++	3
Fluvoxamine	+/0	++	++	++	3

SNRI					
Venlafaxine	+	+	+	++	3
Desvenlafaxine	+	+	+	++	3
Duloxetine	+	+	++	+	4
NRI					
Atomoxetine	+	++	+/0	0	0
NDRI					
Bupropion	++	0	+	0	0
Atypical					
Mirtazapine	+/0	++	0	++	+++
Trazodone[5]	0	+++	0	0	0

Key: +++: substantial side effects; ++: moderate side effects; +: mild side effects; +/0: possible side effects; 0: none

1 This is an acute side effect occurring within a few hours after the first dose of the medication or when there is a dosage increase; includes anxiety and insomnia that can continue during the first two weeks of treatment but often subsides thereafter.

2 Primarily inorgasmia, seen in approximately 25 to 30 percent of patients; can be associated with all SSRIs, venlafaxine, desvenlafaxine, and duloxetine.

3 Acute weight gain is rare. A small percentage (possibly 10 percent) of patients may experience weight gain after being on the medication for 12 months or more.

4 Not yet determined.

5 The low incidence of side effects (except sedation) assumes the use of low doses, e.g., 25–50 mg (see figure 2-D).

Figure 2-E

In addition to prescription antidepressants, two over-the-counter products have demonstrated some efficacy in treating depression: Saint-John's-wort and SAM-e. Although there are a number of outcome studies with these drugs in the treatment of adults with depression, no such studies have been conducted with children or adolescents, and thus they should be considered to be experimental. It should be noted that

Saint-John's-wort has been associated with significant effects on liver metabolism and can adversely interact with other medications, including birth control pills, which it may render ineffective.

Guidelines for the Pharmacological Treatment of Depression

Treatment is started with low doses during the first week (see figure 2-D) and then, if tolerated, gradually increased. A low starting dose is important because approximately 5 percent of children have a condition referred to as "2D6 hypometabolism." This condition causes an inadequate first-pass metabolism of some drugs, including antidepressants, resulting in high blood levels of the drug and, thus, very significant side effects (2D6 is a liver enzyme that is responsible for metabolizing a number of antidepressants and other drugs). Were these children to be started on higher doses, the initial side effects could be overwhelming.

One of the most common problems in initiating treatment is activation, an acute onset side effect that may occur within a few hours after taking the first dose of a drug or when dosages are increased. Patients experiencing activation present with anxiety, initial insomnia, and sometimes agitation. It is important to note that this is different from switching, which occurs when an antidepressant provokes the emergence of mania or hypomania in a person with bipolar disorder. Switching generally does not occur until the medication has been taken for two or more weeks (thus the main differential feature of activation versus switching is the time of onset).

Because activation can be unpleasant, when parents see it they may not only stop the medication but also become afraid of and pessimistic about psychiatric drug treatment in general. Thus, parents need to be warned that activation can happen and, if it does, to contact the doctor right away. Clinicians can also coprescribe a low dose of a minor tranquilizer (such as lorazepam [Ativan], 0.125 mg) and instruct the parents to give it to their child if signs of activation appear. Fortunately, activation generally subsides within one to two weeks. By the end of the first month of treatment, tranquilizers are usually no longer necessary.

The general rule of thumb is to start with a low dose, as mentioned previously, and then increase the dose while carefully watching for signs of either a clinical response or the emergence of side effects (which would suggest that the dose is too high). There are no well-established guidelines for how long to wait between dosage adjustments, although it is common practice to treat for a month to 6 weeks and then to increase the dose if there has been no sign of clinical improvement (generally this is a better first-step strategy than switching to a different drug or adding a second medication). Please also keep in mind that some children are late responders, and there is some positive yield by continuing to treat for a number of weeks until clinical improvement is noted.

If a positive clinical response occurs, then how long does continuation treatment last? The answer to this question has not been clearly determined in efficacy studies. It is well known that in adults and older adolescents it is very important to continue treatment with an antidepressant at the *same dose* for a minimum of 6 months after symptomatic improvement, followed then by gradual discontinuation. This guideline has often been adopted in the treatment of children as well, despite the absence of empirical support for this strategy.

The clinician should be alert to the possible development of two late-onset side effects that can be seen in some patients treated with antidepressants (this is the case for all antidepressants except bupropion): (1) apathy and emotional blunting, and (2) emotional disinhibition, both apparently due to the downstream effect of serotonin on the dopamine neurotransmitter system in the frontal lobes (Barnhart et al., 2004). This often-unrecognized side effect completely subsides with discontinuation of medication or may respond favorably to the coadministration of bupropion (which activates the dopamine system).

Antidepressants and Suicidality

The media have given a good deal of attention lately to the potential risks of antidepressants and their connection to increased suicidality (especially in children and adolescents). The initial concern came from a study in England that raised concerns about increased suicidality in young patients treated with the antidepressant Paxil (paroxetine). In this study, which included 1,300 patients, Paxil was compared to placebo, and reports of increased suicidality were seen in 1.2 percent of placebo- and 3.4 percent of Paxil-treated subjects. This difference is statistically significant. It is important to note that there were no actual suicides in this group of youngsters and that a number of suicidal "events" occurred in the Paxil group when the children *stopped* taking the medication.

In trying to understand and address this issue, we face one significant problem: the concept of suicidality has been very loosely defined in this and other studies. In most cases it includes reports of increased thoughts about suicide, suicide gestures, and non-lethal-intent self-mutilation (as is often seen in people with borderline personality disorders). In one instance, even a report of a child slapping herself qualified as a suicide attempt (Brown University, 2004). Of course, actual suicides and lethal attempts are also included under this umbrella of suicidality.

Concerns regarding increased suicidality have had a significant impact on both the prescribing of antidepressants and parental fears about the use of these drugs. The United Kingdom Committee on Safety of Medications has banned the use of all antidepressants for use in patients under the age of 18, with the exception of fluoxetine (Prozac). In the United States the FDA has also responded to concerns about increased suicidality by requiring drug companies to issue warnings about the use of these drugs with younger clients. They have also initiated a study to investigate the data—an examination of a database of 4,400 teenagers treated with antidepressants—and final conclusions are pending. It is interesting to note that in this large group of adolescents treated with SSRIs there have been no suicides. It has also been documented that in geographic areas where antidepressants are in widespread use, suicide rates have dropped among adolescents (Mahler, 2004).

Even though the likelihood of increased suicidality may be low in large group studies, the clinician must be on the lookout for the emergence of suicidal tendencies in all patients who suffer from major depression. It is certainly possible that in some cases the drug can contribute to this problem. The following may account for increased suicidality seen in some individuals treated with antidepressants:

- Activation and increased restlessness may add to a general sense of emotional discomfort.

- Antidepressants can provoke dysphoric mania in some youngsters who, in fact, have bipolar disorder. (See chapter 3.)

- Increased energy may occur before a decrease in depressive mood (giving the person the energy to carry out a suicide attempt).

- Noncompliance

Noncompliance (patient- or parent-initiated discontinuation) can result in two common, problematic results that might account for increased suicidality: antidepressant withdrawal symptoms (see Medication Discontinuation later in this chapter) and/or the loss of what had been a positive antidepressant effect, plunging the patient back into depression.

What is clear is that untreated major depression carries significant risks of potential suicide. Treatment with antidepressants takes several weeks before the first signs of clinical improvement appear, and depression can worsen during this start-up period of treatment. In evaluating these kinds of concerns we must always differentiate between media hype and scientific data. Refer parents who may be interested in this issue to the NIMH website (www .nimh.nih.gov).

Treatment of Depressive Subtypes

There are several nonblinded studies showing the effectiveness of antidepressants in the treatment of dysthymia in children (Nobile, Cataldo, Marino, & Molteni, 2003). Treating dysthymia is important since without treatment it generally lasts for 3 to 4 years with substantial negative effects on psychosocial functioning and development. Additionally, many if not most children with dysthymia eventually develop major depression. It is unclear whether early treatment of dysthymia can prevent major depression later, although professionals speculate that it can. Obviously, further study is needed to confirm the efficacy of antidepressants in treating dysthymia.

SSRIs are effective agents for treating premenstrual dysphoric disorder (PMDD). (Note that the nonserotonin antidepressants such as NRIs and NDRIs are not effective in treating PMDD.) Unlike patients being treated for other depressive disorders, PMDD patients often have an acute positive response to treatment with SSRIs, possibly showing symptomatic improvement several hours after taking the first dose. Additionally, generally patients need only take the medication for the period of time that they typically experience emotional symptoms, perhaps only a few days every month, thus allowing them to avoid longer-term side effects.

Many severe types of major depression in young people present with psychotic symptoms. Often, psychotic symptoms are not as easy to observe in people with mood disorders as they are in patients with schizophrenia or drug-induced psychosis. Many very depressed youngsters harbor delusional thoughts (for example, somatic delusions) but keep these thoughts to themselves, and clinicians may treat them for months, not appreciating the psychotic aspect of the disorder. Thus it is very important to carefully assess for the presence of these less-obvious signs of psychosis. Psychotic symptoms necessitate the use of antipsychotic medications (in conjunction with antidepressants) or the use of electroconvulsive therapy (ECT). Additionally, the presence of psychotic symptoms should strongly increase one's index of suspicion that the patient has bipolar disorder (see chapter 3).

Medication Discontinuation

Discontinuation withdrawal symptoms have been well documented. These symptoms, which occur with abrupt discontinuation, generally include nausea, body aches, nervousness, insomnia, a peculiar "electrical shock" sensation experienced periodically, and generalized body aches like those that come with a flu-like illness. There have been reports of increased suicidality upon rapid discontinuation, possibly due to one or both of the following factors: either the medication was controlling the depression and, with its discontinuation, it is no longer having this effect, or the distress caused by withdrawal symptoms has provoked the emergence of suicidal feelings. Severe withdrawal symptoms are most likely to be seen in connection with two drugs (both of which have short half-lives): paroxetine and venlafaxine. Withdrawal symptoms can occur with the discontinuation of most other antidepressants as well, with the exception of fluoxetine (with which it occurs very rarely, due to its long half-life). Withdrawal symptoms can generally be avoided if the medication is gradually discontinued over a period of 4 to 8 weeks.

Relapse Prevention

Adults experiencing a third episode of major depression are best treated by ongoing, chronic antidepressant therapy to reduce the likelihood of recurrence. As noted earlier, many if not most children experiencing a major depression will have recurrences. However, inadequate data supports chronic use of antidepressants with youngsters. Thus, until more research is available to address this issue, it is probably prudent to gradually discontinue medications after 6 months of asymptomatic status (as noted above) and educate the patient and his or her parents to watch for signs of possible recurrence. If these signs are spotted, parents should seek treatment as soon as possible.

CHAPTER 3

Bipolar Disorder

For adolescents, the prevalence of bipolar disorder, or cyclothymia, is approximately 1 percent and 5 to 6 percent for subsyndromal symptoms (Lewinsohn, Klein, & Seeley, 1995, 2000; Costello et al., 2002). Many cases of bipolar disorder have their onset in childhood or adolescence. Prepubertal children: 27 percent, teenagers up to the age of 18: 38 percent, and adults: 35 percent (STEP-BD Program, 2008). For many patients, manic symptoms begin during mid-adolescence.

The prevalence of bipolar disorder in young children has not been established due to lack of large-scale epidemiological studies. There is a growing recognition that bipolar disorder does affect children in some cases. However, controversy concerning the prepubertal diagnosis of bipolar disorder remains. Areas of debate include the accurate establishment of the age of onset, implications of comorbid conditions, atypical presentations, and definition of symptom criteria.

DIAGNOSTIC ISSUES

The diagnosis of early-onset bipolar disorder is often difficult to establish, especially in young children. The *DSM-IV-TR* (American Psychiatric Association, 2000) diagnostic criteria are the same for children, adolescents, and adults. However, the symptom presentation in young patients may not be clearly recognizable or may overlap with those of other disorders. Biederman, Birmaher, and Carlson (2000) estimate that only 40 percent of prepubertal patients referred to clinics for evaluation of bipolar disorder meet *DSM-IV-TR* criteria for bipolar I or bipolar II disorder. Several expert consensus groups are seeking to provide desperately needed diagnostic clarity, including developmentally appropriate criteria and instruments, with high interrater reliability and validity. A brief review of various bipolar criteria is provided below.

For a diagnosis of bipolar I, the patient must have had at least one manic or mixed episode, characterized by abnormally elevated or irritable mood, of at least one week in duration (or less if hospitalization was required). Often patients have a history of one or more major depressive episodes. Functional impairment will be evident, as well as 3 or 4 additional symptoms from the following list:

- Grandiosity

- Decreased need for sleep

- Flight of ideas

- Distractibility

- Pressured speech

- Increased activity

- Risk-taking behavior

A mixed episode is defined as at least a one-week period during which the criteria for both a manic episode and a depressive episode (except duration) are met. Mixed episodes are characterized by the following:

- Significant impairment in occupational or social functioning, hospitalization, or psychotic features

- Higher prevalence among young patients

- Dysphoria

- Disorganized thinking or behavior

Bipolar II is diagnosed following at least one hypomanic episode and one depressive episode. Hypomania is a marked, observable, uncharacteristic elevation in mood, lasting at least 4 days, plus 3 or 4 of the symptoms listed above. There is no functional impairment or hospitalization.

Some researchers and clinicians propose modified diagnostic criteria for juvenile-onset bipolar disorder. For example, Liebenluft, Charney,

Towbin, Bhangoo, and Pine (2003) suggest four bipolarity categories for children, with the following definitions:

1. Meets full *DSM-IV-TR* criteria for hypomania or mania, including duration, and displays classic elevated mood or grandiosity

2. Meets symptom criteria for hypomania or mania, but not duration criteria, with episodes 1 to 3 days in length

3. Meets duration criteria, but episodes are characterized by irritability, not euphoria

4. Mood disorder, NOS (not otherwise specified): predominant symptoms are irritability and hyperarousal (not euphoria), which are chronic, not episodic

There are advantages to adopting the expanded spectrum approach, including earlier diagnosis and treatment. However, many experts recommend using caution when deviating from *DSM-IV-TR* criteria, because the disadvantages are misdiagnosis and inappropriate treatments, which in some cases may worsen the clinical course.

Papolos and Papolos (2007) and Coyle et al. (2003) have attempted to address the diagnostic complexities by summarizing how the signs and symptoms of early-onset bipolar disorder may differ from the disorder in adults.

SIGNS AND SYMPTOMS OF EARLY-ONSET MANIA

- Chronic, not episodic
- Mixed states commonly occur with marked dysphoria and irritability
- Severe oppositional behavior
- Ultrarapid cycling
- Explosive outbursts or rage episodes

Carlson, Bromet, and Sievers (2000) provide a useful analysis of early-versus adult-onset psychotic mania. In this study, early-onset subjects were aged 15 through 20 years and adult subjects were defined as over age 30. A higher number of early onset subjects

- were male

- had a history of childhood behavior disorders

- abused substances

- displayed paranoia

- experienced less frequent episode remissions during 24-month follow-up

Bipolar Disorder and Attention-Deficit/ Hyperactivity Disorder (ADHD): Differential Diagnosis

Comorbid conditions include ADHD, anxiety disorders, oppositional defiant disorder, and substance abuse. Determining the bipolar-ADHD boundary in children poses particular diagnostic difficulties and is one of the most challenging differential diagnoses to make. As shown in figure 3-A, the symptom overlap with ADHD and bipolar disorder is significant.

SYMPTOMATIC SIMILARITIES: ADHD AND CHILDHOOD-ONSET MANIA

- Irritability

- Inattention

- Hyperactivity

- Impulsivity

- High level of energy

- Pressured speech

- Chronic and nonepisodic

Figure 3-A

Figure 3-B lists clinical features and other factors that help to differentiate ADHD from bipolar illnesses.

DIFFERENTIATING BIPOLAR DISORDER FROM ADHD

Symptoms Common to Bipolar Disorder but Very Rare with ADHD [1,2]

- Decreased need for sleep without daytime fatigue

- Low morning arousal

- Intense, prolonged rage attacks (lasting 2 to 4 hours)

- Hypersexuality

- Flight of ideas

- Morbid nightmares[2]

- Psychotic symptoms

- Family history of obvious bipolar disorder or one or more of the following in blood relatives:

  - Suicide

  - Severe alcohol or drug abuse

  - Multiple marriages

  - Tendency to start numerous businesses

- Hyperthymia (a form of chronic hypomania characterized by high energy and productivity, gregariousness, impulsive behavior, and decreased need for sleep)

---

1 Geller & DelBello (2003), pp. 25–50

2 Popper (2004)

Figure 3-B

Bipolar Disorder and ADHD: Comorbidity

The association between early-onset bipolar disorder and ADHD continues to be a topic of considerable debate. The major discussion points are summarized below:

- Bipolar and ADHD may represent distinct disease entities.

- In some children with ADHD, the ADHD may be a pro-drome of bipolar disorder. (Most children with ADHD do not go on to develop bipolar illness, and most bipolar patients do not have early ADHD-like symptoms. Thus there may be a subtype of bipolar illness that simply presents with early signs that mimic ADHD.)

- Childhood-onset bipolar disorder may be related to other bipolar spectrum conditions but represent a particular subtype of mood disorder (in other words, it is in some ways different from adult-onset bipolar conditions).

- Comorbid early-onset bipolar disorder and ADHD may constitute a distinct and particularly serious syndrome.

The actual rate of juvenile-onset bipolar disorder and ADHD comorbidity is not firmly established. The reported rate of co-occurrence is high, up to 80 percent for children and 30 percent for adolescents. However, many of the studies have methodological limitations. For example, Geller, Sun, Luby, Frazier, and Williams (1995) examined only rapid cycling and mixed episode patients. Findings reported by Wozniak, Biederman, Mundy, Mennin, and Faraone (1995) were based on a family-focused pilot study. Small sample sizes and retrospective design are limitations found in many studies. Sachs, Baldassano, Truman, and Guille (2000) advise cautious interpretation of results based on retrospective data collection from adults about their childhood symptoms. As mentioned previously, *although symptom overlap does occur*, most children with ADHD do not develop bipolar disorder later in life, and most bipolar patients do not have a history of fully diagnosed ADHD.

Many critical questions remain unanswered. Are the comorbidities actual? Are the co-occurrence rates explained by the symptom overlap between the two disorders? Do the comorbidities represent a progressive or prodromal syndrome? Why is there a disparity in comorbidity rates (higher comorbidity when the primary diagnosis is bipolar disorder and lower rates when the primary diagnosis is ADHD)? Does treatment history contribute to comorbidity (for example, stimulant-induced mania)? Experts raise these questions and acknowledge the inherent limitations in the design and execution of research studies, categorically emphasizing the pressing need to establish diagnostic clarity.

Bipolar Disorder and Anxiety Disorders

The clinician is faced with challenges when diagnosing and treating comorbid bipolar disorder and anxiety disorders. However, there is no comprehensive body of information on the incidence, clinical course, and treatment recommendations and outcomes from which clinicians could obtain guidance. While bipolar disorder is known to coexist with anxiety disorders in children and adolescents, the nature of the overlap has not been determined. The family-genetic findings of Wozniak, Biederman, Mounteaux, Richards, and Faraone (2002) raise questions regarding whether bipolar-anxiety disorder comorbidity is a distinct clinical entity and to what degree anxiety may be a precursor of early-onset bipolar disorder.

Results of a study reported by Masi et al. (2004) point to earlier OCD onset and more severe OCD symptomology in adolescent patients with comorbid bipolar disorder and OCD. Findings of Birmaher et al. (2002) addressed the occurrence and severity of comorbid bipolar disorder and panic disorder. The presence of either panic disorder or bipolar disorder increased the likelihood of co-occurrence of the other. Psychotic symptoms and suicidal ideation were more frequent in youths with bipolar disorder and panic disorder than in patients with other comorbid mood (non-bipolar) and anxiety (non-panic) disorders.

Because of the risk of inducing mania, hypomania, or cycle acceleration, special attention must be paid to medication when treating comorbid bipolar and anxiety disorders. Antidepressants are common treatments in some anxiety disorders, and the potential risks of using these medications when comorbid bipolar disorder is present must be considered.

Bipolar Disorder and Other Comorbidities

Differentiating bipolar disorder from major depression is of critical importance, because 70 percent of cases of early-onset bipolar illness first become manifest in major depression. See chapter 2 for a discussion of the differentiation of major depression from bipolar disorder. As mentioned above, a potential consequence of misdiagnosing bipolar disorder as major depression, and treating with an antidepressant, is the triggering of a manic or hypomanic episode. Additionally, mood instability would persist due to the absence of a mood stabilizer.

In older adolescents, the distinction between bipolar disorder and schizophrenia presents a diagnostic challenge, especially with a first episode of psychotic mania. Because psychotic symptoms and anxiety are relatively common with bipolar onset prior to age 18, the differential diagnosis can be difficult. Misdiagnosing bipolar disorder as schizophrenia may result in the omission of a mood stabilizer from the medication regimen, which would not be beneficial to the patient.

NEUROBIOLOGY

The neurobiology of bipolar disorder is thought to include both functional and structural abnormalities in multiple central nervous system (CNS) locations. A detailed discussion of various pathophysiological models is beyond the scope of this book. However, several areas of interest and research are summarized below.

Abnormalities in Protein-Signaling Networks

These systems can be thought of as similar to cellular cogwheels (Manji, 2001) that serve to regulate cellular input and output. Abnormalities in these pathways are being investigated for their role in bipolar disorder (Bhalla & Iyengar, 1999; Weng, Bhalla, & Iyengar, 1999).

Cellular Resiliency

Neuroprotective proteins, which are thought to mitigate the destructive neurochemical processes in the brain, have been identified. Some mood stabilizer medications increase levels of neuroprotective proteins. Ongoing research seeks to determine whether abnormalities in the levels, or functioning, of neuroprotective proteins are contributory in bipolar disorder (Soares & Mann, 1997; Manji, Moore, Rajowska, & Chen, 2000).

Neurochemical Abnormalities

The role of altered central nervous system biochemical mechanisms, related to cellular resiliency, is another area of study. Research continues to expand, with interest in N-acetylaspartate (NAA), glutamate, GABA, and postsynaptic second messengers. As is the case with bipolar disorder in adults, early-onset bipolar disorder appears to be associated with impairment in the dorsolateral prefrontal cortex, basal ganglia, hippocampus, and cingulate. Recent notable contributions include those of Bertolino et al. (2003); Chang et al. (2003); Chen et al. (2004); and Silverstone, Asghar, O'Donnell, Ulrich, and Hanstock (2004).

Kindling Model

The term *kindling* (Ballenger & Post, 1980) is used to describe a malfunctioning neurochemical process thought to have a role in several psychiatric disorders. The model suggests the presence of cumulative subclinical biochemical alterations in the limbic system. In the presence of these chronic changes, neurons become more excitable, eventually resulting in clinical and observable symptoms. It has been suggested that kindling may explain the longitudinal progression and clinical course patterns characteristic of bipolar disorder.

Genetic and Family Studies

Heritability of bipolar disorder has been demonstrated in familial, twin, and adoption studies (Tsuang & Faraone, 1990). Both genetic and environmental factors are presumed to be important. While no twin or adoption studies specific to pediatric bipolar disorder have been conducted, family studies demonstrate a strong familial component. Though genetic linkage studies are not conclusive, several chromosomes have been investigated. Questions about the distinction between bipolar disorder and schizophrenia have been raised due to the implications of Chromosome 22 in both conditions (Nurnberger & Foroud, 2000; Potash & DePaulo, 2000; Kelsoe et al., 2001).

PSYCHOPHARMACOLOGY

Mood Stabilizers

Pharmacotherapy is the mainstay of treatment of bipolar disorder. This section covers the three commonly used and studied mood stabilizers—lithium, divalproex (Depakote), and carbamazepine (Tegretol)—as well as lamotrigine (Lamictal), a newer agent.

LITHIUM

Lithium is an established mood stabilizer, with 50- to 80-percent response rates for typical bipolar disorder in adults and adolescents. Lithium is a first-line agent indicated for bipolar mania, bipolar depression, and prophylaxis. Lithium is approved by the FDA for use in children 12 to 18 years of age. The mechanism of action is unknown, but it does have effects on multiple CNS components. Current research focuses on lithium's ability to stabilize neurochemical systems, and its neuroprotective effects. Despite the efficacy of lithium, dosing requirements, side effects, and monitoring parameters may limit its use in pediatric patients.

Lithium is prescribed based on dosing recommendations, symptom response, and blood levels. Lithium demonstrates a narrow therapeutic index—the therapeutic dose is very close to the toxic dose. Therefore, blood tests are required, which may limit use in pediatric patients. The onset of action of lithium is 5 to 14 days, although full symptom resolution may take up to several months.

The side effects of lithium occur along a continuum, ranging from benign and transient to fatal toxicity. Common side effects include increased thirst, increased urination, nausea, vomiting, diarrhea, headache, cognitive slowing, tremor, weight gain, and worsening of acne. More serious, although less common, effects are changes in kidney function, hypothyroidism, cardiac conduction abnormalities, and increased white blood cell count.

Anticonvulsant Medications

Divalproex and carbamazepine are anticonvulsant medications that have demonstrated efficacy in the treatment of bipolar disorder. Both of these agents are widely used to treat seizure disorders in pediatric patients. A newer agent, lamotrigine, is less widely prescribed, both as an anticonvulsant and mood stabilizer. The mechanism of action of anticonvulsants in bipolar disorder is unknown. Among the properties of anticonvulsants are stabilization of cell membrane ion channels, potentiation of the inhibitory neurotransmitter GABA, and inhibition of the excitatory neurotransmitter glutamate. In addition, several anticonvulsants demonstrate neuroprotective properties, as does lithium.

DIVALPROEX

Divalproex is a first-line agent for mania and considered to be the preferred drug for mixed episodes. Opinions differ on whether it is the preferred drug for rapid cycling. Divalproex is FDA approved for bipolar mania in adults. Common side effects are nausea, vomiting, drowsiness, and weight gain. Less common, but more serious, are liver damage, pancreatitis, tremor, hair loss, blood clotting disorders, and polycystic ovary disease. Routine blood level monitoring is required for divalproex, utilizing anticonvulsant ranges. Toxic levels of divalproex are potentially life threatening.

CARBAMAZEPINE

Carbamazepine is a second-line agent for mania. Common side effects include nausea, vomiting, dizziness, drowsiness, and rash. Less common, but more serious, are liver damage, cardiac abnormalities, and decreases in red and white blood cell counts.

Carbamazepine is known to interact with multiple medications, requiring additional testing for drug levels and dosage adjustments. Routine blood level monitoring is required for carbamazepine, utilizing anticonvulsant ranges. Toxic levels of this anticonvulsant are potentially life threatening.

LAMOTRIGINE

Lamotrigine is a first-line agent for bipolar depression in adults. Common side effects include nausea, vomiting, constipation, ataxia, and skin rash. A serious dermatological side effect called Stevens-Johnson syndrome is associated with lamotrigine, especially when used in combination with divalproex. Children are more at risk for developing this reaction than adults. Benign rash, a common side effect of lamotrigine, is not initially distinguishable from the more serious form. Patients and family members should be instructed to report any signs of rash to their physician.

Although other anticonvulsants, including gabapentin (Neurontin), oxcarbazepine (Trileptal), and topiramate (Topamax), are prescribed or mentioned in professional literature, to date there is a lack of evidence to support their routine use to treat bipolar disorder.

Guidelines for the Pharmacological Treatment of Bipolar Disorder

Despite the fact that information is accumulating regarding treatment of early-onset bipolar disorder, only recently have experts begun issuing treatment guidelines (Kowatch et al., 2005). Most recommendations are based on case reports and open-label studies. There remains a critical need for definitive guidelines based upon rigorous clinical drug trials that provide reliable information about safe and effective medication treatment for juvenile-onset bipolar disorder (Carlson et al., 2003). As is the case with adults, biological therapies for children include the use of mood stabilizers, lithium, and anticonvulsants, antipsychotics, and ECT. Treatment should be aimed at the stabilization of initial presenting target symptoms, full syndrome resolution, and relapse prevention.

The section below offers treatment guidelines for the phases (mania and depression), associated symptoms (agitation and psychosis), and comorbidities (ADHD and anxiety) of bipolar disorder.

MANIA

Lithium, divalproex, and atypical antipsychotics (e.g., quetiapine) are first-line agents. Therapy with a combination of mood stabilizers should be considered after careful evaluation; the majority of children with mania may ultimately require treatment with two or more mood stabilizers in combination to achieve a good outcome (Kowatch et al., 2000; Emslie & Mayes, 2001; Geller & DelBello, 2003; Findling et al., 2003).

Olanzapine (Zyprexa) was the first atypical antipsychotic to be FDA approved as monotherapy for acute manic or mixed episodes. The APA recommends using olanzapine only in less-severe episodes. The FDA has either approved or is reviewing expanded indications, including mono-therapy, for other atypical antipsychotics (clozapine (Clozaril), risperi-done (Risperdal), quetiapine (Seroquel), and aripiprazole (Abilify)).

DEPRESSION

There is general consensus that antidepressants are not effective in treating bipolar disorder and can actually worsen the condition (for example, by causing switches into mania and/or increasing the frequency of episodes). Currently there are five options for treating bipolar depres-sion: (1) quetiapine (Seroquel); (2) lamotrigine (Lamictal) (can be used to treat adolescents, but caution is warranted in treating children owing to rare but dangerous side effects; such as severe rashes including Stevens-Johnson syndrome); (3) lithium (Eskalith), if given in doses large enough to achieve a blood level of at least 0.8 mEq/L; (4) olanzapine-fluoxetine combination (Symbyax); and (5) ECT (electro-convulsive therapy) for very severe, psychotic, and/or highly treatment-resistant cases.

SEVERE AGITATION AND SLEEP DISTURBANCE

Short-term use of benzodiazepines is recommended, and atypical antipsychotics are preferred.

PSYCHOSIS (IF PRESENT)

Atypical antipsychotics are preferred.

COMORBID ADHD AND BIPOLAR DISORDER

Initiate treatment with mood stabilizer(s). Once stability has been achieved, stimulants may be added gradually.

COMORBID ANXIETY DISORDERS AND BIPOLAR DISORDER

Use SSRI antidepressant, when medications are indicated, with careful titration and monitoring.

More-detailed drug information regarding first- and second-line mood stabilizers—lithium, divalproex, and carbamazepine—is provided in figure 3-C. See chapter 2 for a detailed discussion of antidepressants and chapter 5 for more information about antipsychotics.

Manic Switching

Current evidence provides conflicting information about the exact occurrence of manic switching and cycle acceleration with the use of antidepressants and stimulants. Experts have not determined precise risk factors in particular patient populations or disorders. Therefore, monitoring for mania or hypomania should be routine. Activation and disinhibition occur with antidepressants, and these side effects need to be differentiated from mania or hypomania.

Drug	Typical Daily Dose	Side Effects
Lithium	C: 15–30 mg/kg/day in 3 or 4 divided doses A: 600–1800 mg/day in 3 or 4 divided doses (or 2 divided doses for sustained-release products)	Sedation, thirst, GI intolerance, tremor, weight gain in 30 to 40 percent of patients, hypothyroidism, headache, cognitive impairment, increased urination, acne, EKG changes, seizure Children under 6 years old may experience more side effects. Contraindicated in pregnancy
Divalproex (Depakote)	C and A: 10–60 mg/kg/day in 2 or 3 divided doses	Sedation, dizziness, drowsiness, blurred vision, lack of coordination, GI intolerance, rash, abnormal blood clotting, weight gain, hair loss, tremor, liver damage, pancreatitis, polycystic ovary disease
Carbamazepine (Tegretol)	C: 10–20 mg/kg/day in 3 or 4 divided doses A: 400–800 mg/day in 2 or 3 divided doses	Sedation, dizziness, drowsiness, blurred vision, lack of coordination, GI intolerance, rash, decrease in red and white blood cell count, cardiac abnormalities

Figure 3-C

Relapse Prevention

Presently only a small body of literature describes the longitudinal course of bipolar disorder in children. In a 2-year follow-up study Geller et al. (2002) reported that only 65 percent of patients reached full syndrome recovery, and 55 percent of those subjects ultimately relapsed. Biederman et al. (2003) reported similar results. Based on suggested remission types (Keck et al., 1998), Biederman et al. estimate that only 20 percent of bipolar youth had achieved functional remission or euthymia (normal, nondepressed mood) after 10 years. These sobering statistics reinforce the necessity of providing early and adequate treatment and ensuring compliance. Patient and family education should emphasize the necessity of long-term treatment. Mood stabilizers are considered to be maintenance therapy in bipolar disorder; antidepressants and antipsychotics are time-limited therapies specific for target symptoms.

Current discussion regarding early-onset bipolar disorder focuses less on its existence and more on diagnostic parameters and treatment options. Awareness of early-onset bipolar disorder is definitely on the increase. Some experts are even questioning whether the pendulum has swung too far: Is the diagnosis of childhood bipolar disorder being made too freely? Or is bipolarity being caused by the liberal prescribing of stimulants and antidepressants in children and adolescents? These are questions worth pursuing, and we include them for purposes of broadening the discussion. However, we aim to focus on the three themes common to both sides of the debate, detailed below.

First, it is generally accepted that bipolar disorder in juveniles is more severe than it is in adults. Early-onset bipolar disorder can have a negative impact on social functioning, school performance, and developmental progress. Second, underrecognition and inappropriate treatment leads to prolongation of intense suffering, may contribute to disease progression, and does not mitigate the suicide risk that may accompany adolescent bipolar disorder. Third, medications used to treat juvenile bipolar disorder are not innocuous and polypharmacy is common, underscoring the need for rational and careful use of these agents. All of these factors point to the importance of making an accurate diagnosis, selecting appropriate medications, and closely monitoring for therapeutic benefit and side effects.

Drug	Interactions with Drugs Commonly Used in Pediatrics	Monitoring Parameters
Lithium	Increased lithium levels: ■ Nonsteroidal anti-inflammatory agents ■ Metronidazole (Flagyl) Decreased lithium levels: ■ Theophylline Neurotoxicity*: ■ Antipsychotics ■ TCAs ■ SSRIs ■ Carbamazepine	Serum levels: Acute mania: 0.8–1.5 mEq/L Maintenance: 0.6–1.2 mEq/L EKG, CBC, electrolytes, renal function tests, thyroid function, weight
Divalproex (Depakote; DVP)	Erythromycin increases DVP levels. DVP increases levels of TCAs. DVP decreases levels of buproprion. Risk of serious rash is increased when DVP and lamotrigine are taken together. Variable effect on levels of other anticonvulsants when taken with DVP.	Serum levels: 50–150 mcg/ml CBC, platelets, liver function, weight

Carbamazepine (Tegretol; CBZ)	Neurotoxicity*: ■ Lithium CBZ decreases levels/ effectiveness of: ■ TCAs ■ Antipsychotics ■ Oral contraceptives ■ Doxycycline	Serum levels: 8–12 mcg/ml CBC, EKG, liver function, weight

* Although neurotoxicity can occur, it is infrequent and does not contraindicate combinations of lithium with the medications listed.

Figure 3-D

CHAPTER 4

Anxiety Disorders

Affecting 5 to 18 percent of children, anxiety disorders are the most common psychiatric conditions in children. These disorders result in significant academic and social impairment and often persist into adulthood. (It should be noted that anxiety disorders are frequently comorbid with bipolar disorder and attention-deficit/hyperactivity disorder, or ADHD.) In this chapter, we focus primarily on obsessive-compulsive disorder (OCD), since among the childhood anxiety disorders OCD is one of the most well researched and one in which pharmacotherapy is a standard treatment strategy. We also provide basic information about other anxiety disorders that may respond to medications.

DIAGNOSTIC ISSUES

Obsessive-Compulsive Disorder

The lifetime prevalence rate of OCD is 2.5 percent for adults and 1 to 2 percent for children and adolescents. OCD usually begins in adolescence or early adulthood, although it is estimated that up to one-third of cases appear before puberty. The gender-specific modal pattern for age of onset is 6 to 15 years for males and 20 to 29 years for females. With childhood onset, the disorder is more common in boys than in girls (3:2). In adults the gender ratio is 1:1. Onset is usually gradual and the course of the disorder is chronic with a waxing and waning pattern.

Symptoms of OCD include recurring obsessions (persistent and intrusive thoughts, ideas, or images that cause marked anxiety or distress) and compulsions (repetitive behaviors intended to reduce obsession-related anxiety). To meet *DSM-IV-TR* (American Psychiatric Association, 2000) criteria for a diagnosis of OCD, the obsessions and compulsions must be so time-consuming (more than one hour per day) or intrusive that normal routines, occupational functioning, or relationships are impaired (Criteria A). Obsessive thoughts are distinguishable from simple worry about everyday problems. Frequently people with OCD avoid situations that involve obsessional content, such as public restrooms due to fear of contamination. They may feel driven to perform the compulsive behaviors, often according to rigid rules. Because there is intense shame, guilt, and secretiveness associated with OCD, diagnosis is difficult and often delayed.

In adults, at some point during the course of the disorder, and with varying degrees of insight, they recognize the obsessions and compulsions to be excessive and unreasonable (Criteria B). Note that Criteria B is not a required diagnostic feature in children as they do not possess sufficient cognitive awareness.

Common obsessions involve fears about disease and contamination, doubt, ordering, aggressive impulses, and sexual imagery. Associated compulsions include hand washing, cleaning, checking, ordering, and mental acts such as silently counting or repeating words.

Childhood and adult OCD presentations are generally similar. In children, washing, checking, and ordering rituals and fear of catastrophe are particularly common. Compulsions without obsessions may occur in children, but generally not in adolescents. Parents may become participants in their children's OCD rituals, especially when responding to reassurance-seeking behaviors, a form of verbal checking.

In a small subset of juvenile patients OCD is associated with streptococcal infections such as scarlet fever or strep throat. The acronym PANDAS (pediatric autoimmune neuropsychiatric disorders associated with streptococcal infections) is used to identify this subgroup of the disorder. The proposed pathophysiology is a post-infection inflammatory process resulting in neuron damage in the basal ganglia. Characteristics include prepubertal onset, neurological abnormalities, and abrupt onset. (For a detailed review of this OCD subtype, see Snider and Swedo [2004].)

Panic Disorder (With or Without Agoraphobia)

The lifetime prevalence rate for panic disorder is 1 to 2 percent. Childhood onset is rare, with typical age of onset between late adolescence and mid-thirties. Panic disorder is characterized by recurrent, unexpected panic attacks and persistent worry and/or behavioral changes associated with additional attacks. Because panic disorder is so rare in children, emergence of panic attacks or panic-like symptoms may be an indication of severe psychosocial stressors, warranting an appropriate evaluation.

Social Phobia (Also Known as "Social Anxiety Disorder")

Lifetime prevalence rates range from 3 to 13 percent for social phobia (or "social anxiety disorder"). Prevalence reports may be upwardly affected by survey parameters, especially when fear of public speaking is included. The usual age of onset is in the mid-teens, often following a childhood history of social inhibition or shyness. Onset may be abrupt or insidious.

In social phobia, the sufferer experiences an intense fear of social situations, leading to anxiety and self-consciousness about being judged, criticized, or rejected. Social situations are very distressing or may be avoided entirely. Anticipatory anxiety and panic attacks are associated features. This anxiety disorder may result in failure to achieve, low self-esteem, and social isolation in children. The anxiety may manifest itself through crying, tantrums, and freezing or shrinking from social situations. Diagnostically in children, the symptoms must occur in peer settings, not just with adults.

Specific Phobias (Formerly Known as "Simple Phobias")

Lifetime prevalence rates for specific phobias (formerly called "simple phobias") range from 5 to 12 percent. Initial symptoms usually occur in childhood, especially with the situational type, natural environment type, animal type, and blood-injection type.

A specific phobia is an enduring and unreasonable fear of a specific object or situation that usually poses little or no danger. Exposure causes immediate anxiety to the sufferer, who finds the object or situation very distressing and may avoid it entirely. Anticipatory anxiety and panic attacks are associated features. When children present with significant specific phobias, clinicians must always look carefully for underlying comorbidities, which are seen in the majority of cases (Walkup, 2004).

Generalized Anxiety Disorder

The lifetime prevalence rate for generalized anxiety disorder (GAD) is 5 percent, with 50 percent of patients reporting childhood onset. GAD is characterized by excessive and exaggerated worry about every-day events. Anxiety and dread are so prominent as to interfere with daily functioning, including work and social activities. Physical symptoms are common and include muscle tension, headaches, nausea, sweating, increased heart rate, insomnia, and exaggerated startle response.

Post-Traumatic Stress Disorder

The lifetime prevalence rate for post-traumatic stress disorder (PTSD) is 8 percent, with onset at any age, usually within the first 3 months after a traumatic event. However, delayed onset may occur months or years later. PTSD develops when (1) an event involving serious physical harm occurred, was threatened, or was witnessed, and (2) the response involved fear, helplessness, or horror.

Typical reactions to traumatic events include shock, anger, anxiety, fear, and guilt. For people without PTSD these reactions abate over time. With people suffering from PTSD these symptoms continue, or increase, and interfere with functioning.

PTSD symptomatology falls into three general clusters:

- Reliving: Examples are flashbacks, disturbing dreams, and intrusive recollections. In children, repetitive play, event reenactment, or frightening dreams that do not directly refer to the traumatic event may be seen.

- Persistent avoidance and limited responsiveness: Efforts are made to avoid thoughts, activities, or places associated with the event. The sufferer may feel a sense of estrangement from others and have a restricted affective range. Children may have a sense of foreshortened future and a general withdrawal from normal life activities.

- Hyperarousal: Initial insomnia, hypervigilance, irritability, concentration problems, and exaggerated startle response may be seen. Children may experience stomachaches and headaches.

Separation Anxiety Disorder

Prevalence estimates for separation anxiety disorder are approximately 4 percent in children and young adolescents. (This disorder occurs only in childhood and adolescence.) When separated from home or primary attachment figures, the child demonstrates social withdrawal, apathy, and sadness. School avoidance may develop. Fear, anger, and attention-seeking behavior may also occur. Symptoms may wax and wane.

Inhibited Temperament

While not a *DSM-IV-TR* disorder, inhibited temperament is a genetically linked temperamental style (Biederman et al., 2001; Schwartz, Snidman, & Kagan, 1999; Kagan, 1998) that affects 10 to 15 percent of children and is characterized by the following behaviors or traits:

- Fear or withdrawal in unfamiliar situations

- Timidity and shyness

- Behavorial inhibition

- Hypervigilance

- Autonomic arousal

- Association with a significant anxiety disorder later in life in approximately 30 percent of children with this temperament

NEUROBIOLOGY

Neurobiology of Obsessive-Compulsive Disorder

Current theoretical models strongly support a neurobiological basis for OCD. The factors listed below support this theory.

Familial Loading

There is a higher concordance rate in monozygotic twins than in dizygotic twins. There is a higher incidence of OCD in first-degree relatives than in the general population (7 percent versus 2.5 percent). Familial loading also exists for OCD and tic disorders.

Basal Ganglia

The basal ganglia function as sensory gates to regulate attention shifting and cognitive aspects of behavior. Theorists have posited that basal ganglia dysfunction in OCD results in an inability to change the focus of attention and leads to the development of perseveration. The development of the PANDAS subtype of OCD aligns with this theory.

Frontal Lobes

It is believed that the frontal lobes inhibit urges and instinctive behaviors arising from more primitive brain structures. Theoretically, in OCD this inhibitory mechanism fails, resulting in the emergence of behaviors associated with more primitive human capacities and territorial preoccupations, such as checking, washing, and ordering. Supporting this theory are several studies that have shown increased metabolic activity in the frontal lobes of OCD patients. Further, frontal lobe pathology typically manifests with inflexibility, stereotypy, and decreased response inhibition, all characteristics of OCD.

MALADAPTIVE NEURAL PATHWAYS

Multiple pathways located in the basal ganglia, prefrontal cortex, cingulate, and caudate are likely involved in the development of OCD (Rosenberg et al., 2004; Russell et al., 2003; Saxena et al., 2003; Baxter et al., 1992; Baxter, 1991). Conceptual models of OCD incorporate neuropsychological deficits, dysfunctional beliefs, and learning or memory disruptions (Tolin, Abramowitz, Kozak, & Foa, 2001; Deckersbach, Otto, Savage, Baer, & Jenike, 2000). Stress or worry leads to intrusive thoughts, which produce exaggerated anxiety signals. Neutralizing behaviors are performed, but the patient does not perceive confirmation of neutralization, despite evidence to the contrary. The ritualistic behaviors persist and increase to the point of perseverated compulsions.

PHARMACOLOGICAL TREATMENT EFFECTIVENESS

The pattern of extremely selective response to medications in OCD is strongly suggestive of biological etiology. Certain antidepressants are highly effective and very selective for serotonergic activity. It is interesting to note that all antiobsessional agents have antidepressant activity, but the converse is not true. Also, unlike many other conditions, OCD shows virtually no placebo response.

Neurobiology of Other Anxiety Disorders

While there is no defining theory about anxiety disorders, most theories incorporate neuroanatomy with a genetic predisposition toward exaggerated responses to environmental or traumatic events. Other than OCD, the anxiety disorder that is perhaps the most widely studied from an etiologic perspective is panic disorder (PD).

One neuroanatomical hypothesis for PD (Gorman, Kent, Sullivan, & Coplan, 2000) is built upon the framework of a central nervous system fear mechanism. One intriguing aspect of this theory attempts to explain how both medications and cognitive behavioral therapy (CBT) can be effective in PD. Central to the fear-network concept is the function of the amygdala, which receives sensory input from the cortex, the brain stem, and the sensory thalamus. The amygdala coordinates autonomic and behavioral responses to the stimulus via the following efferent projections:

- Locus coeruleus: increases norepinephrine release, results in physiological and behavioral arousal

- Periaquaductal gray area: mediates defensive behaviors, postural freezing

- Parabrachial nucleus: causes increased respiration

- Hypothalamic paraventricular nucleus: activates the HPA axis and release of adrenocorticoids (e.g. cortisol)

- Hypothalamic lateral nucleus: activates the sympathetic nervous system

From afferent pathways, the amygdala also receives information from the higher level cortical regions involved in processing and evaluating sensory input. It is hypothesized that in panic disorder neurocognitive deficits in these cortical pathways lead to misinterpretation of the sensory information. A misguided context is created, resulting in heightened amygdala activity as well as hyperexcitability of downstream efferent regions.

Once encoded by the amygdala, the hippocampus then stores this faulty information and conveys it to the amygdala upon reexposure. These stored memories are very resistant to extinction and subject to generalization, and so stimuli that resemble the triggering event may elicit intense anxiety.

At the cellular level, in the locus coeruleus, serotonin is inhibitory. SSRIs effectively increase synaptic concentrations of serotonin. It is postulated that the antipanic effects of SSRIs result from inhibition of hyperreactivity of the amygdala, in turn resulting from increased serotonin activity.

The effectiveness of CBT in PD is thought to be related to effects upstream from the amygdala. Decreasing cognitive distortions, reducing abnormal emotional reactions, and reducing phobic avoidance are believed to enhance the ability of the prefrontal cortex to inhibit the amygdala.

Another naturally occurring biochemical substrate for anxiety is gamma-aminobutyric acid (GABA), which reduces brain excitability.

GABA promotes the passage of chloride ions into the nerve cells and makes them less excitable. The receptor complex to which GABA molecules bind also contains a receptor site to which benzodiazepines (BZs) attach. Benzodiazepines (minor tranquilizers such as Ativan and Xanax) are effective antianxiety medications. It is hypothesized that a naturally occurring equivalent to these medications exists in the brain, although it has not yet been identified. In theory, the individual tendency to be more, or less, affected by stressful situations could be linked to a deficit, or abundance, of this naturally occurring chemical.

Many of the tenets of the fear-network concept related to PD may be applied to separation stressors or social phobias. It has been suggested that the infant's locus coeruleus is triggered and hyperaroused during infant-caregiver separation. There may be experiential similarities or a common substrate between phobic rejection sensitivities and abnormal separation reactions. The study of the expanding efficacy of SSRI antidepressants across a range of anxiety disorders may shed more light on these issues.

PSYCHOPHARMACOLOGY

Pharmacology of Obsessive-Compulsive Disorder

SSRI antidepressants are first-line agents in the treatment of OCD. Substantial evidence supports the use of citalopram, fluoxetine, fluvoxamine, paroxetine, and sertraline. Clomipramine, a TCA with serotonergic activity, is also highly effective in treating OCD. The relative side effect profiles of an SSRI and clomipramine are often the determining factors in agent selection.

Response rates range from 50 to 75 percent, characterized by a gradual response pattern (Walkup, 2004; Cook et al., 2001; Thomsen, Ebbesen, & Persson, 2001).

Time Course	Symptom Reduction
6 to 10 weeks	25 to 30 percent
18 to 24 weeks	40 to 50 percent
52 weeks>	50 percent
Figure 4-A	

Generally, doses used to treat OCD are higher than those needed to treat depression. In figure 4-B, dosages are provided for medications currently approved by the FDA for use in pediatric OCD.

Generic Name	Brand Name	Initial Dose	Daily Dose
Citalopram	Celexa	C/A: 10 mg	C/A: 10–60 mg
Clomipramine*	Anafranil	C/A: 25 mg daily	C/A: 200 mg/ day or 3 mg/ kg/day, which- ever is lower
* FDA indication for children and adolescents			
Fluvoxamine*	Luvox	C/A: 25 mg at bedtime	C/A: 50–200 mg/day (Higher dosages divided)
* FDA indication for ages 8–17 years			
Fluoxetine*	Prozac	C: 10 mg daily A: 10 mg daily	C: 10 mg/day A: 20 mg/ day (also higher-weight children)
* FDA indication for ages 7–17 years			

Sertraline*	Zoloft	C: 25 mg daily A: 50 mg daily	C: 25–200 mg/ day A: 50–200 mg/ day
* FDA indication for ages 13–17 years			
Figure 4-B			

Guidelines for the Pharmacological Treatment of OCD

Pharmacotherapy for adult and pediatric OCD is solidly established, with similar response rates to medications for adult and pediatric OCD patients. Adequate dosages for extended periods of time are required. For adults, CBT is a well-documented intervention and response rates approach 90 percent. The most effective treatment for adult OCD combines medications with CBT.

The specific type of CBT employed in OCD includes exposure and response prevention. In this process the patient is gradually and systematically exposed to the anxiety-provoking stimuli but is not allowed to engage in the associated rituals. Initially, the experience is very difficult for the patient, but over time the drive to perform the rituals diminishes. Unfortunately, the technique is time consuming and not readily available to all patients.

Until recently, the evidence-based efficacy of CBT in childhood OCD relative to, or in combination with, medication was unclear. However, the Pediatric OCD Treatment Study (POTS), a 2004 multi-center NIMH-funded research endeavor, has provided clarity. Findings from this study suggest that treatment for pediatric OCD begin with CBT alone, or CBT combined with an SSRI. Further studies are needed to examine long-term outcomes and treatment guidelines.

Results from the POTS underscore the importance of CBT as a short-term treatment intervention in pediatric OCD. In clinical practice, only a small percentage of children receive a recommended CBT protocol (March, Franklin, Nelson, & Foa, 2001). Most are placed on an SSRI as monotherapy. When adequate symptom response is not seen, the SSRI is sometimes augmented with a clomipramine or atypical antipsychotic, exposing the child to inappropriate polypharmacy. Starting with CBT alone may eliminate the need for additional SSRIs.

Psychopharmacology of Other Childhood Anxiety Disorders

At this time the most convincing evidence to support medication treatment in other childhood anxiety disorders comes from the landmark Research Unit on Pediatric Psychopharmacology Anxiety study (2001). In this multicenter, randomized, double-blind, placebo-controlled study conducted by a university-based research network, the safety and efficacy of psychiatric medications in pediatric patients was investigated. Anxiety symptom reduction was noted in 76 percent of the fluvoxamine subjects, with an effect size of 1.1 (one of the highest seen with any pediatric psychiatric disorder). The robust findings from this study strongly suggest a role for fluvoxamine in the short-term treatment of generalized anxiety disorder, social phobia, and childhood separation anxiety disorder (the authors also suggest that similar results are seen with other SSRIs, although fluvoxamine was the medication used in this study). Further studies are needed to replicate these very promising findings, and to amass a sufficient body of evidence from which to construct best-practice guidelines. Benzodiazepines also have a limited role in therapy, for short-term treatment when a child refuses to go to school or shows certain specific phobias, such as fear of dental or medical procedures.

Despite the lack of numerous evidence-based studies, clinicians often utilize SSRI antidepressants to treat a variety of childhood anxiety disorders, and all SSRIs appear to be effective in treating panic disorder, social phobia, and generalized anxiety disorder. When SSRIs are prescribed, initial dosages should be low, with a slow titration. For most childhood anxiety disorders, psychotherapy, including CBT, is the treatment of choice. However, psychopharmacological treatment of anxiety disorders in children is a rapidly emerging area of interest and more findings will likely be published in the near future.

CHAPTER 5

Psychotic Disorders

Although psychotic disorders present relatively infrequently in child-hood, they are usually a harbinger of lifelong illness. The most common diagnoses are schizophrenia and bipolar disorder, which together have an incidence of 1 to 2 percent in adolescents. Both of these disorders presage chronic medication treatment. These conditions are the most severe and are therefore most likely to require prompt pharmacological treatment to avoid serious consequences such as suicide.

DIAGNOSTIC ISSUES

Psychosis itself is not a diagnosis but a symptom. The term *psychotic* is defined in *DSM-IV-TR* (American Psychiatric Association, 2000) in somewhat differing ways depending on the diagnosis, but it is usually used to refer to the presence of hallucinations and/or delusions. Historically the term has been defined, in the *DSM-III-R*, as "gross impairment in reality testing and the creation of a new reality" (American Psychiatric Association, 1987). Although a number of symptoms can be seen in the context of psychotic disorders, impaired reality testing is the central defining feature. Impaired reality testing may be seen in the form of bizarre behavior; however, it is most clearly observed in patients' verbal output and content of speech; psychotic patients reveal false beliefs (delusions) and seriously impaired perceptions (hallucinations). Thus, depending on the person's age, psychotic symptoms may be more difficult to assess and detect in children, since they may be demonstrated only in their behavior, not in their verbalizations. You will note that the definition involves not only impairment of reality testing, which alone would simply lead to confusion, but also the "creation of a new reality," such as delusions ("I am being followed by a monster") or hallucinations ("I hear a voice telling me I am bad").

TYPES OF CHILDHOOD PSYCHOTIC DISORDERS

Childhood psychotic disorders can be divided into three main groups: schizophrenia and related disorders, psychosis related to a mood disorder, and psychosis related to a medical disorder or substance.

Schizophrenia

Schizophrenia is a disorder that has been recognized since the time of Hippocrates. It can start during adolescence, or, rarely, during childhood. A disorder previously called "childhood schizophrenia" included what is now considered autism (see chapter 7).

The clinical picture of schizophrenia varies depending on the particular phase of the disorder. The *DSM-IV-TR* divides the course of schizophrenia into three phases: prodromal, active, and residual.

During the prodromal phase, patients show deterioration in their level of functioning, or a failure to develop normally, without being actively psychotic. In this phase, the patient may show mostly "negative" symptoms (discussed below), such as a tendency toward isolation, blunted or flat affect, lack of initiative, and possibly a disruption of sleep patterns. Often the patient's school performance and personal hygiene deteriorate. This phase may last for months or years in children, making diagnosis difficult.

During the active phase, the patient shows psychotic symptoms with disorganized thinking, delusions, and hallucinations.

In the residual phase, the patient continues to be impaired, but without florid psychotic symptoms. To warrant a diagnosis of schizophrenia, these three phases together must last at least six months. Schizophreniform disorder has the same criteria as schizophrenia, but its duration is less than six months. Three types of schizophrenia are delineated: catatonic (prominent movement disorder), disorganized (severe thought disorder), and paranoid (prominent paranoid delusions with mild disorganization of thinking). Those cases that do not fit into the above three types but have a mix of features may be categorized as undifferentiated or residual types.

For practical purposes, it is helpful to group schizophrenic symptoms into four categories, as outlined below. (Note that the characterological features are not psychotic symptoms by themselves but often accompany the core positive or negative symptoms.)

POSITIVE SCHIZOPHRENIA SYMPTOMS

- Hallucinations
- Delusions
- Agitation
- Floridly bizarre behavior

NEGATIVE SCHIZOPHRENIA SYMPTOMS

- Anhedonia
- Apathy
- Blunted affect
- Poverty of thought
- Feelings of emptiness
- Amotivational states

DISORGANIZATION SCHIZOPHRENIA SYMPTOMS

- Behavioral disorganization
- Distractibility
- Thought disorder

CHARACTEROLOGICAL SCHIZOPHRENIA SYMPTOMS

- Social isolation or alienation
- Marked feelings of inadequacy
- Poorly developed social skills

Other psychotic disorders include the following:

- Brief psychotic disorder: symptoms lasting less than one month, usually with an identifiable stressor
- Delusional disorder: persistent nonbizarre delusions
- Schizoaffective disorder: episodes of mania and/or depression in addition to the symptoms of schizophrenia
- Shared psychotic disorder: symptoms developing as a result of intense relationship with someone who is already psychotic

Psychotic Mood Disorders

Both depression and mania can present in children and adolescents with psychotic symptoms. Usually these are mood congruent delusions or hallucinations. For example, depression may be accompanied by auditory hallucinations saying the person is bad or deserves to die, and mania may be accompanied by grandiose delusions. These are discussed in more detail in chapters 2 and 3.

Psychosis Associated with a Medical Condition

Psychotic symptoms can be substance induced, or they can be related to a medical condition. Hallucinogens such as lysergic acid diethylamide (LSD), phencyclidine (PCP), and stimulants such as amphetamines or ecstasy can produce psychotic symptoms during intoxication. Alcohol and sedative-hypnotics can produce psychotic symptoms during withdrawal.

NEUROBIOLOGY

Over the centuries, a multitude of theories have been used to explain the etiology of schizophrenia, ranging from religious and social to psychological and biological. The dopamine model has been accepted as the predominant theory of biological causation for the past two decades. This model holds that the basic physiological pathology involves primarily overactive or hyperreactive dopamine neurons. The excessive dopamine activity can lead to behavioral agitation, a failure to adequately screen stimuli, and disorganization of perception and thought. This theory is supported by two observations. The first is that the potency of antipsychotic drugs, until the atypicals, has correlated closely with their ability to bind to and block the postsynaptic dopamine (D2) receptors in the mesolimbic system. The second observation is that drugs that increase dopamine activity (such as amphetamines) can produce a paranoid psychosis similar to paranoid schizophrenia and, if given to schizophrenic patients, may exacerbate psychotic symptoms. However, several lines of evidence, including the fact that the newer atypical antipsychotics are weak dopamine (D2) blockers, have indicated that the dopamine theory does not fully explain the etiology. Newer theories suggest involvement of serotonin and glutamate systems. It does appear that the underlying pathology remains latent until the brain matures during adolescence, at which time the symptoms become manifest.

PSYCHOPHARMACOLOGY

There are two main types of antipsychotic medication: first-generation antipsychotics, also called neuroleptics (which include the phenothiazines), and the newer atypical antipsychotics (second-generation antipsychotics). These two classes of medications have significant differences, which are described below. In general, the second-generation antipsychotics offer major benefits in the treatment of schizophrenia and psychosis related to a mood disorder. Psychosis related to a medical condition can be treated with a traditional antipsychotic. Other factors to consider include the following:

- If an antipsychotic medication has been used with success in the past, generally the same medication is again prescribed.

- The patient's motor state is important to bear in mind. Typically, very agitated patients may be given a more-sedating medication (such as Seroquel), whereas markedly regressed or withdrawn patients will be given a less-sedating drug (for example, Abilify).

- The side-effect profile of the drug chosen must be considered in relation to the individual patient's profile. For example, some of the atypical antipsychotics have a strong tendency to produce weight gain (discussed below) and should be avoided when treating a child who is obese.

Side Effects of Antipsychotic Medications

EXTRAPYRAMIDAL SIDE EFFECTS

Antipsychotics produce extrapyramidal side effects (EPS) due to the blocking of dopamine receptors. In addition to producing a reduction in positive psychotic symptoms by blocking dopamine in the mesolimbic region, unfortunately they also produce extrapyramidal symptoms by blocking dopamine in the basal ganglia. The acute extrapyramidal symptoms are manifested as follows: (1) Parkinsonian side effects resembling symptoms of Parkinson's disease, with slowed movements, decreased facial expression, resting tremor, and a shuffling gait; (2) dystonic symptoms, which involve sustained muscle spasms, usually of the neck or shoulder (such as torticollis), and can be quite frightening and painful; and (3) akathisia, an intense feeling of restlessness. At times akathisia may be confused with psychotic agitation and lead to an increase in medication dosage—resulting in increased akathisia. Severe akathisia can be very uncomfortable and is associated with increased noncompliance and risk of suicide. Antipsychotic medications, especially those that have high potency, can cause neuroleptic malignant syndrome (NMS), a potentially fatal neurological condition that is considered a severe form of EPS.

ANTICHOLINERGIC

Antipsychotic medications block acetylcholine receptors and thereby affect the parasympathetic nervous system, leading to dry membranes (particularly of the mouth and eyes), blurred vision (especially of nearby objects), intestinal slowing (constipation), difficulty initiating urination, and sedation.

ANTIADRENERGIC

Antipsychotic medications produce alpha-adrenergic blockade, which leads to orthostatic hypotension. This means that when the child stands up, blood pressure drops significantly, leading to transient light-headedness and potential injuries resulting from falls.

TARDIVE DYSKINESIA

All of the above-listed side effects appear within the first few hours or days of treatment or with increases in dose. In contrast, the tardive dyskinesias (disorders involving involuntary movements) appear late in the course of treatment or when the medication is reduced or discontinued. These movements usually lessen slowly over time, but they may persist for years even after the medication is discontinued. Patients should be routinely examined for this using the Abnormal Involuntary Movement Scale (AIMS) or other scale. The risk of tardive dyskinesia is significantly lower with the newer atypical antipsychotics.

METABOLIC

Recent concern about the use of the second-generation antipsychotics has focused on their tendency to produce weight gain, due to an alteration of carbohydrate metabolism similar to diabetes, and an alteration of lipid metabolism. In some cases this was not discovered until the patient developed diabetic coma, a potentially fatal condition. Also, the diabetes did not always resolve after the medication was discontinued. The elevation of serum lipids may lead to an increased risk of heart disease and stroke. The magnitude of this risk was discussed at a joint conference of the American Diabetes Association, American Psychiatric Association, and the American Association of Clinical Endocrinologists (2004). The members of these organizations concluded that clozapine and olanzapine appear to have significant metabolic effects, risperidone and quetiapine appear to have moderate metabolic effects, and ziprasidone and aripiprazole appear to have minimal metabolic effects (although they have been less studied). They recommend that all patients on these medications should have their weight, blood sugar, and lipid levels monitored.

ANTIPSYCHOTIC MEDICATIONS				
Generic Name	Brand Name	Initial Dose (mg)	Daily Dose (mg)[1]	Equivalence (mg)
Low Potency	First Generation			
Chlorpromazine	Thorazine	10	150–375	100
Mesoridazine	Serentil	10	100–325	50
Thioridazine	Mellaril	10	100–325	100
High Potency	First Generation			
Fluphenazine	Prolixin	1	1.5–10	2
Haloperidol	Haldol	0.5	1–10	2
Loxapine	Loxitane	5	50–100	10
Molindone	Moban	5	25–100	10
Perphenazine	Trilafon	2	6–22	10
Pimozide	Orap	0.25	1–5	1
Thiothixene	Navane	2	4–20	5
Trifluoperazine	Stelazine	1	2–15	5
Second Generation				
Aripiprazole	Abilify	5	10–20	10
Clozapine	Clozaril	6.25	100–450	50
Iloperidone	Fanapt	2	12–24	10

Olanzapine	Zyprexa	1.25	5–15	2
Paliperidone	Invega	1	12	1–2
Quetiapine	Seroquel	12.5	100–550	50
Risperidone	Risperdal	0.25	0.5–4	1
Ziprasidone	Geodon	5	40–140	10

1 Doses appropriate for both children and adolescents.

Figure 5-A

SIDE EFFECTS OF ANTIPSYCHOTIC MEDICATIONS

Medication	Sedation	Extrapyramidal	Anticholinergic
Low Potency	**First Generation**		
Chlorpromazine	++++	++	++++
Mesoridazine	++++	+	+++++
Thioridazine	++++	+	+++++
High Potency	**First Generation**		
Fluphenazine	+	+++++	++
Haloperidol	+	+++++	+
Loxapine	+	+++	++
Molindone	+	+++	+++
Perphenazine	++	+++	++
Pimozide	+	+++++	+
Thiothixene	+	++++	++
Trifluoperazine	+	++++	++

Second Generation			
Aripiprazole	+	+/0	0
Clozapine	++++	0	+++++
Iloperidone	+	+	+/0
Olanzapine	++	+/0	+
Paliperidone	+	+	+/0
Quetiapine	++	+/0	++
Risperidone	+	+	+/0
Ziprasidone	+	+	+

Key: +++: substantial side effects; ++: moderate side effects; +: mild side effects; +/0: possible side effects; 0: none

Figure 5-B

Guidelines for the Pharmacological Treatment of Psychotic Disorders

Because the child's psychotic behavior may be putting him or her in danger, paying attention to the child's safety in the initial evaluation is crucial. The clinician may determine that the patient needs hospitalization or other measures to ensure his or her safety. It is important to work with the family in this regard and to address any precipitating stressors. Antipsychotic medications should be considered at the first sign of psychotic symptoms, including disorganization of behavior. Often prompt initiation of treatment can help avoid the development of a more florid psychosis. Early intervention is important because psychosis is associated with increased suicide risk, and some evidence suggests that the longer a person is psychotic, the more difficult it becomes to treat the psychosis (Loebel et al., 1992). The presence of delusional thinking, hallucinations, severe manic symptoms, or disorganized behavior suggests a need for antipsychotic medication.

The first step in the initiation of treatment is to choose a medication, as discussed previously. The medication can then be started at a low dose, usually given at bedtime. The dose is then gradually increased until a good response is achieved or side effects become intolerable. If an effective dose is not tolerable, the clinician should try a new medication that would minimize the problematic side effects. For example, if the first medication produces severe EPS, a medication with low incidence of EPS should be tried. Medication should be continued for at least one year after a psychotic episode, with the exception of schizophrenia, which should be treated with medication on an ongoing basis. When the diagnosis is schizophrenia, discontinuing the medication at any time is likely to lead eventually to relapse.

Relapse Prevention

Once the acute psychosis has been treated and the child's condition has stabilized, in most cases the medication dose can be gradually decreased to about half of the acute dose. Medications should usually be continued for at least twelve months. For schizophrenia and schizoaffective disorder, the risk of relapse is significantly reduced by continuing medication treatment. If the condition deteriorates or psychotic symptoms return, medication should be promptly reinstituted or increased.

CHAPTER 6

Attention-Deficit/ Hyperactivity Disorder

Attention-deficit/hyperactivity disorder (ADHD) affects approximately 5 percent of children. As they mature neurologically, most teenagers with ADHD experience a noticeable reduction in motoric restlessness or hyperactivity, but the core symptoms of ADHD (impulsivity, impaired attention, and lack of intrinsic motivation) continue through adolescence and on into adulthood. Most experts agree that about 40 percent of children with ADHD completely outgrow the disorder by early adulthood (likely due to the ongoing maturation of the prefrontal lobes, which may continue until the late twenties or early thirties). Of those with ADHD, 60 percent experience ongoing symptoms throughout life.

Medical treatments for ADHD are considered to be very effective, as we shall address below. Unfortunately, epidemiological studies have shown that approximately 5 percent of children meet criteria for ADHD, but only 13.6 percent of these have received treatment (Pliszka et al., 2000). Untreated ADHD results in considerable accumulated disability, and rates of co-occurring substance abuse, anxiety, and depression are quite high.

DIAGNOSTIC ISSUES

It is very important to emphasize the fact that most psychiatric disorders appearing in childhood present with some degree of motoric restlessness and inattention. Thus, these outwardly observable behaviors do not automatically lead to a diagnosis of ADHD. Figure 6-A lists those disorders that must be considered in any comprehensive evaluation of children with hyperactivity and inattention.

DIFFERENTIAL DIAGNOSIS OF CHILDHOOD-ONSET PSYCHIATRIC DISORDERS PRESENTING WITH HYPERACTIVITY AND INATTENTION

- Diffuse brain damage (such as that commonly seen in fetal alcohol syndrome, following a head injury, and so on)

- Anxiety disorders

- Agitated depression

- Situational stress

- Bipolar mania or hypomania

- Prepsychotic conditions

- Impaired affect regulation associated with severe early abuse or neglect

- Boredom (especially likely in bright children who are academically understimulated)

Figure 6-A

The diagnosis of ADHD is based largely on three sources of data: a detailed family history (since ADHD is considered to be a genetically transmitted disorder and thus often runs in families), a very careful history detailing the nature and onset of behavioral symptoms, and a description of current symptoms (especially as they vary across situations). It is also a diagnosis of exclusion; one must always first rule out those disorders listed in figure 6-A.

The most common presentation for ADHD is an early onset, often in infancy, of restlessness, unstable sleep patterns, and affective lability (especially with excessive crying and difficulty being soothed). In most children, ADHD is identified when they enter preschool—where they experience their first sustained contact with other children and encounter social standards and expectations. Most experts agree that this *very early onset* of significant behavioral problems is characteristic of ADHD. However, emerging data suggests that some children destined to have bipolar disorder *may* show early-onset behaviors that are similar to ADHD (for example, prodromal symptoms of bipolar disorder; see chapter 3).

During childhood the following ADHD symptoms predominate: hyperactivity, impulsivity, impaired self-control, difficulty staying on task, and limited intrinsic motivation to stay focused, especially on mundane, nonexciting, or low stimulus value tasks. Such symptoms are often highly context dependent; that is, they are most noticeable in situations where the child is required to remain still and quiet, such as in the classroom, yet they may not be as noticeable in an environment that is inherently exciting, novel, or stimulating, such as when playing a video game.

With adolescence, as noted above, motoric hyperactivity is often reduced, but core symptoms remain. Disorganization, which may manifest itself in the form of messy lockers, notebooks, and bedrooms, is often pronounced in the ADHD adolescent, as are increasing problems adapting to societal and school-related demands for independent task performance and self-control. Additionally, rates of substance abuse are high, especially among untreated ADHD adolescents.

It is important to note that the so-called "inattentive type" of ADHD appears to be a totally unrelated neurological disorder. Children with this disorder do show impaired attention, but they are not hyperactive or impulsive. This fundamental difference is also underscored by the failure of stimulants to treat the inattentive subtype (except in rare instances). Unfortunately, to date, there are no highly effective medical treatments for this inattentive subtype.

NEUROBIOLOGY

Numerous studies of metabolic functioning suggest impaired frontal-lobe functioning in people suffering from ADHD. In addition, abnormalities have been shown in the dopamine neurotransmitter system. For this reason, dopamine agonists such as stimulants and bupropion are effective at reducing ADHD symptoms. Minor structural abnormalities have also been found in the brains of ADHD subjects, specifically smaller cerebellar volumes, smaller volumes of frontal and temporal areas, and a smaller caudate nucleus.

Appropriate treatment with stimulants may not only reduce symptoms but also normalize the chemical microenvironment of the developing brain and ensure more-normal brain maturation. Castellanos et al. (2002) demonstrated that ADHD children have smaller cerebral and cerebellar volumes than age-matched controls. The degree of reduction in frontal, temporal, cerebellar, and white matter volumes correlated significantly with parent and teacher ratings of ADHD symptom severity. Unmedicated ADHD subjects exhibited strikingly smaller white matter volumes compared to both controls and ADHD children treated with stimulants. This suggests that appropriate pharmacological treatment may contribute to more-normal brain development, and in this respect medication treatments may be neuroprotective.

PSYCHOPHARMACOLOGY

Three classes of medications have been shown through empirical methods to be effective in the treatment of ADHD: stimulants, certain antidepressants, and alpha-2 adrenergic agonists.

Stimulants

Of the more than one hundred randomized controlled trials of stimulant treatment of ADHD, the results are very consistent: stimulant treatment of ADHD has a high degree of efficacy, with robust effect sizes ranging from 0.8 to 1.0 (Pliszka et al., 2000).

The action mechanism of stimulants is inhibition of dopamine reuptake (additionally, amphetamines promote increased release of dopamine from presynaptic vesicles). Figure 6-B lists currently available stimulants (with doses appropriate for both children and adolescents). There are different ways to categorize stimulants, either by the onset of action or by the duration of action. In general, most of these agents have a rapid onset of action, with symptom reduction occurring 30 to 60 minutes after ingestion, and a duration of action ranging from 4 to 12 hours (although most provide adequate symptom relief for only up to 6 hours). Depending on the formulation, dosing takes place two or three times daily, with some long-acting products requiring only once-daily dosing. It is most important to find the best possible dose and dosing schedule for a given patient.

IMMEDIATE RELEASE STIMULANTS (duration of effect is 3 to 6 hours)		
Generic	**Brand**	**Typical Daily Dose**
Methylphenidate	Ritalin	10–60 mg
	Metadate	10–60 mg
	Methylin	10–60 mg
	Concerta	18–54 mg
Dexmethylphenidate	Focalin	5–20 mg
Dextroamphetamine	Dexedrine	5–40 mg
Lisdexamphetamine	Vyvanse	30–70 mg
Amphetamines	Amphetamine mixed salts (Adderall)	5–40 mg
	Methamphetamine (Desoxyn)	5–25 mg
SUSTAINED RELEASE STIMULANTS (duration of effect is 6 to 12 hours)		
Methylphenidate	Ritalin SR	20–60 mg
	Ritalin LA	20–60 mg
	Metadate ER	10–60 mg
	Metadate CD	20–60 mg
	Methylin ER	20–60 mg
	Concerta	18–54 mg
	Daytrana (patch)	15–30 mg
Dextroamphetamine	Dexedrine spansules	5–40 mg
Amphetamine	Adderall XR	5–40 mg
Figure 6-B		

Of children with ADHD, 38 percent appear to respond equally well to all stimulants; however, 62 percent have been shown to respond better to one specific stimulant than to others (Greenhill et al., 1996). What this means is that, although the stimulants are similar in their impact on the nervous system, differences do exist. Thus, if the results of a trial of one stimulant (such as methylphenidate) are less than optimal, then it is advisable to conduct a trial using another stimulant (such as dextro-amphetamine). When systematic trials are conducted using each of the three classes of stimulants, good outcomes are seen in about 90 percent of accurately diagnosed ADHD patients (Barkley, 2000).

Guidelines for the Pharmacological Treatment of ADHD

STIMULANTS

Superior treatment outcomes were demonstrated in a large-scale study (MTA Cooperative Group, 1999). Keys to successful treatment were shown to be the following: (1) start with low initial doses of stimulants; (2) carefully titrate the dose up to adequate levels; (3) dose three times a day initially, then moving to once or twice a day once an optimal dose is determined; (4) monitor for side effects; and (5) provide close follow-up. As noted above, stimulants produce noticeable symptomatic improvement 30 to 60 minutes after being ingested; thus it is often possible to determine within a few days or a week which dose is most appropriate for any given child. Many children are treated for ADHD by their pediatricians, and close follow-up is rare, especially in managed-care settings. However, it is crucial, for optimal outcomes, to provide close supervision, especially during the first few weeks of treatment. If it is not possible for the clinician to see patients once a week, frequent telephone contact during the first few weeks of treatment can be very helpful. Additionally, it is important to monitor drug responses by using standardized rating scales that are completed each week by both the child's teacher and the parents (for example, using the Conners Global Index for Parents and for Teachers [Conners & Barkley, 1985]).

It is generally best to begin medication treatment during the weekend. Because the effects of stimulants generally have a duration of 4 to 6 hours, if treatment is started on a school day the benefits of the medication may be noticed by teachers but will have worn off by the time the child returns home. Thus, the parents will not see the benefits and will be unable to provide an accurate assessment of the drug's effects. In fact, during the hour or two after the drug has been eliminated from the patient's body there may be an actual increase in symptoms (this is referred to as "medication rebound"). As a result, the parent may witness only the problematic rebound behavior and decide to discontinue treatments.

There is general agreement among ADHD experts that stimulants should be used every day, not just on school days. ADHD, in addition to having a marked negative impact on academic performance, also results in significant problems in social interaction. Appropriate, consistent stimulant treatment can significantly improve a child's social competency, peer acceptance, emotional interactions with family members, and self-esteem. Most children successfully treated with stimulants will require ongoing medication well into adolescence and possibly into adulthood. Stimulants are well tolerated and are considered to be the safest and have the mildest side effects of all psychiatric drugs. The most common side effects are initial insomnia (especially if administered after 4:00 p.m.), reduced appetite, stomachaches, mild dysphoria, lethargy, and headaches. These side effects are usually easily managed (see figure 6-C).

STIMULANT SIDE EFFECTS AND SOLUTIONS	
Side Effect	**Solutions**
Initial insomnia	Try earlier dosing, or coadminister clonidine or trazodone given at bedtime.

Reduced appetite (Generally only affects the patient when the drug is active; it has not been associated with significant problems obtaining adequate nutrition. Thus the side effect is generally not treated.)	If necessary, switch to Focalin, which may result in less of this effect.
Stomachache	Give medications with food.
Mild dysphoria	Switch classes of stimulants, or add an antidepressant such as bupropion.
Lethargy, sedation, or impaired concentration (Generally indicates that the dose is too high.)	Reduce dose.
Headache	Reduce dose, or change stimulants.
Figure 6-C	

Experts disagree regarding tics, ADHD, and stimulant treatment. ADHD and tics frequently co-occur (in both treated and untreated ADHD). In some instances stimulants *may* exacerbate (but not cause) tics, even though in comparison studies the rate of tics seen in children treated with stimulants and placebos is not significantly different. Despite this fact, clinicians should tell parents that tic symptoms may increase but in most instances are not caused by the medication. Tics are commonly treated by the coadministration of alpha-2 adrenergic agonists (see below and also chapter 8).

Comorbid anxiety disorders are common in children with ADHD. Stimulants can, at times, exacerbate anxiety. However, guidelines published by the Texas Department of Mental Health (Pliszka et al., 2000) recommend that, in cases of comorbid ADHD and anxiety, stimulants be used first. Often children's anxiety is associated with social and academic failure, and the anxiety subsides if the ADHD is successfully treated with the stimulants. In cases where anxiety increases significantly with a stimulant trial, it is a common practice to administer an SSRI or venlafaxine.

Many parents are understandably concerned about the use of stimulants since they can be abused. It is important to openly discuss this issue with all parents. The fact is that rates of substance abuse in untreated ADHD patients are indeed quite high, yet research clearly demonstrates that the use of stimulants to treat ADHD actually significantly reduces the risk of substance abuse in ADHD patients (Biederman et al., 1999; Hechtman & Greenfield, 2003).

One of the major drawbacks of stimulants is that they only work for a short period of time and the positive effects wear off in the late afternoon. And when stimulants are taken after 4:00 p.m., they commonly cause initial insomnia. This limitation presents a challenge, because ADHD symptoms can adversely affect patients in the late afternoon and evening, in the form of behavioral problems, family conflicts, or difficulty concentrating on homework. Thus, coadministration of antidepressants or alpha-2 adrenergic agonists (see below) may be an option for targeting symptoms later in the day.

Mistaking other disorders for ADHD and treating these with stimulants can have highly adverse consequences (see figure 6-D, below).

CONSEQUENCES OF MISDIAGNOSIS AND SUBSEQUENT STIMULANT TREATMENT

Correct Diagnosis	Consequences
Anxiety disorder	Increased anxiety
Agitated depression	Increased agitation
Preschizophrenia	Psychosis
Bipolar disorder	Increased manic symptoms *Possible* cycle acceleration
Situational stress	Failure to address psychological issues

Figure 6-D

ALPHA-2 ADRENERGIC AGONISTS

Clonidine (Catapres) and guanfacine (Tenex) may be used to treat core ADHD symptoms (see figure 6-E); however, they are more effective in reducing irritability, aggression, and impulsivity and promoting sedation (to treat initial insomnia). Alpha-2 agonists are also the treatment of choice for comorbid tics.

ALPHA-2 ADRENERGIC AGONISTS		
Generic	**Brand**	**Typical Dose**[1]
Clonidine	Catapres	0.15–0.4 mg[2]
Guanfacine	Tenex	0.25–1.0 mg[3]
1 Doses appropriate for children and adolescents.		
2 Three to four times a day		
3 Two to three times a day		
Figure 6-E		

Combined use of alpha-2 agonists and stimulants is a common practice, both for treating ADHD and comorbid ADHD and tics (Walkup, 2004). Although four cases of death in children taking clonidine in conjunction with a stimulant have been reported, the FDA conducted an investigation and failed to find any significant cause for concern over the coadministration of these drugs. The deaths occurred in children with very complicated medical problems, and the FDA concluded that the drugs were not a causal factor in the deaths.

ANTIDEPRESSANTS

Of children with ADHD, 20 percent will experience co-occurring depression. Antidepressants certainly may be helpful in reducing mood symptoms. However, certain classes of antidepressants have also been shown to have positive effects on core ADHD symptoms. Not all antidepressants should be used to treat ADHD—only those that increase the availability of dopamine or norepinephrine. Thus, SSRIs, although often a good adjunct for treating anxiety or depression, are not effective in treating core ADHD symptoms. In fact, as mentioned in chapter 2, a later-onset side effect of SSRIs can be disinhibition; when this occurs in patients being treated for ADHD, it can result in an increase in impulsivity and occasionally aggression. SSRIs are not contraindicated in the treatment of comorbid anxiety or depression, but the clinician must be watchful for this possible complication. Antidepressants that have evidence of efficacy in treating ADHD are listed in figure 6-F. (Note that tricyclic antidepressants have been found to be effective in treating ADHD; however, due to significant side effects and toxicity, these are not generally drugs of choice. In some treatment-resistant cases nortriptyline can be used as an alternative.)

ANTIDEPRESSANTS USED TO TREAT ADHD		
Generic	**Brand**	**Typical Daily Dose**
Bupropion	Wellbutrin SR/LA	C: 100–150 A: 150–300 mg
Atomoxetine	Strattera	1.2–1.8 mg/kg (same for children and adolescents)
Figure 6-F		

Treatment outcomes with antidepressants for ADHD symptoms are not as robust as those seen with stimulants; however, they afford several advantages:

- Once-a-day dosing

- No need for triplicate prescription

- No addiction potential

- Effects (generally seen within 5 to 40 days after initiating treatment) typically last 24 hours and thus cover evening hours

- Can be used to treat comorbid depression

Antidepressants generally require a low starting dose and a gradual increase over the first 3 weeks of treatment. Although some positive effects can be seen in the first 1 to 3 weeks, achieving the full effect may require 3 months of ongoing treatment.

COMBINED BEHAVIORAL TREATMENT AND PSYCHOPHARMACOLOGY

The MTA study demonstrated that medication treatment alone was equally effective as behavioral treatment and that the combination of both treatment modalities provided only modest benefits beyond the use of each treatment separately (MTA Cooperative Group, 1999). However, in most cases the ideal treatment is to use both medication and psychological approaches to manage core ADHD symptoms. And certainly psychotherapy (family and/or individual) can be very helpful in treating comorbid anxiety or depression.

CHAPTER 7

Autism Spectrum Disorders

The autism spectrum disorders, also known as "pervasive developmental disorders" (PDD), are often seen as a range of disorders, with autistic disorder as the most severe form. Other disorders include Asperger's disorder, Rett's disorder, childhood disintegrative disorder, and pervasive developmental disorder not otherwise specified. These disorders have various degrees of dysfunction in three main areas: social interaction, communication, and repetitive behaviors. The incidence of autism seems to be increasing. A review of recent surveys suggests the rate of all PDDs is about 60 per 10,000 and the prevalence of autism is about 13 per 10,000 (Fombonne, 2005). Boys are three to four times more likely than girls to have autism. Autistic disorder was originally thought to be more common in upper socioeconomic classes, but more recent studies suggest that this was due to referral bias. Currently, these disorders are under intense investigation due to their prevalence and lack of effective specific treatments. It is hoped that a better understanding of them will lead to a clearer comprehension of the relationship between the brain and behavior.

DIAGNOSTIC ISSUES

Autism

Autism (a common term used to refer to both autism and autistic disorder) was originally described by Kanner, in 1943, who gave it the name *early infantile autism* and identified two main features: autistic aloneness and obsessive insistence on sameness. Since then, several revisions have been made to the diagnostic criteria. The current diagnostic criteria as described in the *DSM-IV-TR* (American Psychiatric Association, 2000) require impairment in the areas of social interaction, communication, and stereotyped behavior, as listed below:

1. Significant impairment in social interaction such as the following:

   - Impairment in the use of nonverbal behaviors such as facial expression in social interaction

   - Failure to develop peer relationships appropriate to age

   - A lack of spontaneous seeking to share interests with others

2. Significant impairments in communication as shown by at least one of the following:

   - Delayed or absent development of spoken language

   - In individuals with adequate speech, impaired ability to converse with others

   - Use of language in stereotyped or idiosyncratic ways

   - Lack of make-believe play or imitative play appropriate to age

3. Stereotyped patterns of interests and activities, as shown by at least one of the following:

   - Intense preoccupation with one or more stereotyped and restricted patterns of interest

   - Rigid adherence to nonfunctional routines or rituals

   - Stereotyped and repetitive motor mannerisms

   - Intense preoccupation with parts of objects

A number of rating scales are used to screen for and diagnose autistic disorder: the Autism Behavior Checklist (ABC), Autism Diagnostic Observation Schedule (ADOS), Autism Screening Questionnaire (ASQ), Autism Spectrum Screening Questionnaire (ASSQ), Checklist for

Autism in Toddlers (CHAT), Childhood Autism Rating Scale (CARS), and Autism Diagnostic Interview (ADI).

Autism is considered the most severe of the pervasive developmental disorders and needs to be differentiated from Asperger's disorder, Rett's disorder, childhood disintegrative disorder, and other developmental disorders such as mental retardation and developmental language disorders. The distinguishing features will be discussed below. In addition, autism is often associated with other disorders. It appears to be most closely related to anxiety disorders, so anxiety, fears, sleep problems, and obsessive-compulsive symptoms are common. Also, attentional problems, hyperactivity, self-injurious behavior, and tics are fairly common.

Asperger's Disorder

Asperger's disorder is often considered a mild form of autism, first described by Hans Asperger in 1944 (Asperger, 1944/1991). In Asperger's, as in autism, there is impairment in social relationships and repetitive and stereotyped patterns of behavior, but minimal delay in language development. People with Asperger's are interested in social relationships but are socially clumsy and insensitive to others. Distinguishing between high-functioning autism and Asperger's can be difficult. The following are the *DSM-IV-TR* diagnostic criteria for Asperger's disorder:

1. Qualitative impairment in social interaction, as manifested by at least two of the following:

   - Impairment in the use of nonverbal behaviors such as facial expression in social interaction

   - Failure to develop peer relationships appropriate to age

   - Lack of spontaneous seeking to share interests with other people

   - Lack of social or emotional reciprocity

2. Stereotyped patterns of interests and activities as shown by at least one of the following:

   - Intense preoccupation with one or more stereotyped and restricted patterns of interest

- Rigid adherence to nonfunctional routines or rituals

- Stereotyped and repetitive motor mannerisms

3. The disturbance causes clinically significant impairment in social, occupational, or other important areas of functioning.

4. No clinically significant delay in language is seen.

Rett's Disorder

Rett's Disorder was first described by Rett in 1966 (Rett, 1977/1966). A condition characterized by its developmental course and development of neurological and behavioral symptoms, it has been linked to mutations in the gene encoding X-linked methyl-CpG-binding protein 2 (MECP2) and is seen almost exclusively in females. There are several types of mutations of the MECP2 gene, but the relationship between type of mutation and clinical presentation is unclear at this time. The disorder does not show any symptoms until after the age of 5 months. Subsequently, patients develop stereotyped hand movements, impaired social interaction, lack of coordination, and impaired language development. Following are the *DSM-IV-TR* diagnostic criteria:

1. All of the following:

- Apparently normal prenatal and perinatal development

- Apparently normal psychomotor development through the first 5 months after birth

- Normal head circumference at birth

2. The following appear after the period of normal development:

- Reduced head growth between 5 and 48 months

- Loss of previously acquired hand skills between ages 5 and 30 months and the development of stereotyped hand movements

- Early loss of social engagement (although social interaction may develop later)

- Development of poorly coordinated gait or trunk movements

- Severely impaired language development with slowed movements

Rett's disorder is associated with abnormal sleep patterns, cardiac and respiratory abnormalities, epilepsy, a variety of behavioral and emotional problems, and increased mortality (Kerr, Armstrong, Prescott, Doyle, & Kearney, 1997).

Childhood Disintegrative Disorder

This disorder was first described by Heller and has been referred to as "Heller's syndrome." Children with this disorder develop normally until at least age 3 or 4 years and then, sometimes following encephalitis, deteriorate over a period of weeks or months. They show significant loss of language ability, social skills, intellectual functioning, and bowel or bladder control and develop repetitive movements and mannerisms. After a period of deterioration, they stabilize and do not show further loss of function. The disorder is seen mainly in males and is rare.

Pervasive Developmental Disorder Not Otherwise Specified

This category includes children who show significant impairment of social interaction and communication but do not fit into any of the above diagnostic categories.

PATHOPHYSIOLOGY

The pathophysiological basis for the PDDs is unclear at this time. Some researchers favor the idea that these disorders are a result of disturbance in affective development. They argue that these children lack the ability to recognize emotional cues. Other researchers propose that the PDDs are a result of abnormal cognitive development. According to this idea, children with these disorders lack the ability to develop a "theory of mind," the ability to attribute thoughts, feelings, and desires to oneself and other people (Baron-Cohen, Leslie, & Frith, 1985). Of course, these theories are not mutually exclusive. Children with these disorders show a variety of abnormalities on neurocognitive tests and brain images, but no clear, consistent abnormality has been found. At one time it was thought that autism was related to thimerosal-containing vaccines such as MMR (measles, mumps, and rubella). Thimerosal, which contains mercury (a known neurotoxin), was used as a preservative in these vaccines. This theory has since been disproven (Hviid, Stellfeld, Wohlfahrt, & Melbye, 2003).

PSYCHOPHARMACOLOGY

Guidelines for the Pharmacological Treatment of Pervasive Developmental Disorders

The treatment of PDDs involves a team approach. It is important that parents and other caregivers, educators, speech therapists, occupational therapists, psychologists, doctors, and psychiatrists all work together closely. The main part of the habilitation process involves behavioral and educational interventions. Medication is used mainly to control symptoms sufficiently to allow the interventions to progress.

There is no effective medication treatment specific to any of the autism spectrum disorders. Certain types of medications have been shown to sometimes be beneficial in the treatment or control of associated symptoms of the PDDs. These are discussed below.

SEROTONIN MEDICATIONS

A type of medication commonly used in the treatment of the PDDs is the group of serotonin antidepressants, including the SSRIs and clomipramine. These medications are often helpful in reducing aggression, agitation, ritualistic behavior, and anxiety and improving social relatedness. These medications are discussed in detail in chapter 2.

ANTIPSYCHOTICS

These medications are also often used in the treatment of PDDs. They can be helpful in reducing aggression and agitation and improving social relatedness. Because of the risk of the development of tardive dyskinesia with long-term use of the earlier versions of antipsychotics, the second-generation antipsychotics may be a better choice. In particular, risperidone has been shown to improve social relatedness, repetitive thoughts, and behavior (McDougle, Holmes, Carlson, Pelton, & Price, 1998; Purdon, Wilson, Labelle, & Jones, 1994). Although the results have been encouraging, some evidence indicates that children may be more sensitive to extrapyramidal and cardiac side effects and weight gain. These medications are discussed in detail in chapter 5.

BETA-BLOCKERS

These medications are considered antihypertensives and are effective in reducing blood pressure because they block one type of norepinephrine receptor. They have been reported to reduce aggression, impulsivity, and self-injurious behavior (Cohen, Tsiouris, & Pfadt, 1991). Similarly, clonidine, a medication that also reduces blood pressure, has been shown to have a calming effect.

MOOD STABILIZERS

There may be some role for lithium and anticonvulsants (valproate and carbamazepine) in the control of agitation and aggression. These medications are discussed in detail in chapter 3.

STIMULANTS

These medications are sometimes helpful in the treatment of attentional problems in children with a PDD. Because of the risk of increased agitation and excitability, they must be used with caution, and usually in low doses. Stimulants should be used only when the child has a generalized problem with distractibility, and not when the distraction is due to preoccupation with some type of ritualistic behavior. These medications are discussed in detail in chapter 6.

OPIOID ANTAGONISTS

Some reports have indicated that naltrexone, an opiate blocker, may be effective in reducing restlessness and improving focus (Kolmen, Feldman, Handen, & Janosky, 1995), but controlled studies have not shown consistent benefit (Campbell et al., 1993).

OXYTOCIN

Oxytocin is a hormone that has been found to influence social bonding. There are experimental studies using oxytocin (injectable or administered via nasal infusion [nasal spray]) that show some promise in improving social recognition and learning (for example, enhancing the ability for autistic individuals to learn to recognize emotional facial expressions). This line of research is very promising, but at the time this book goes to press, the use of oxytocin is still considered to be experimental.

MISCELLANEOUS AGENTS

The intense interest in autism and related disorders has stimulated much research into potentially effective treatments. Currently the main approach to treatment is to use medications appropriate to the associated conditions, such as an SSRI when there are prominent obsessive-compulsive symptoms. The following treatments have been proposed, but without sufficient evidence to support their efficacy:

- Secretin, a gastrointestinal hormone

- Digestive enzymes

- Levetiracetam, an anticonvulsant, reported to reduce hyper-activity, impulsivity, mood instability, and aggression

- Donezepril, a cholinesterase inhibitor used in the treatment of Alzheimer's disease, reported to reduce irritability and hyperactivity

- Thiamine tetrahydrofurfuryl (TTFD), proposed due to its ability to counteract the effect of heavy metals, such as mercury in thimerosal

- Carnosine, a dipeptide with neurological activity

- Lofexidine, an alpha-adrenergic receptor partial agonist similar to clonidine, shown to have some benefit in reducing hyperactivity

- Tianeptine, to reduce irritability in children with autistic disorder

Initiating Treatment

The initial choice of medication should be based on the type of symptoms that are interfering most with the child's habilitation progress. Once these symptoms are identified, a medication can be chosen. It should be started at a low dose and monitored closely for effects, both positive and negative.

CHAPTER 8

Miscellaneous Disorders

In this chapter we will discuss several disorders more briefly. These are disorders that are less common or less severe and/or have a a biological basis that is less clear than that of others. They include Tourette syndrome, conduct disorder, eating disorders, and substance-use disorders.

TIC DISORDERS AND TOURETTE SYNDROME

Tourette (or Gilles de la Tourette) syndrome (TS) affects an estimated 5 to 10 in 10,000 children and is characterized by motor and vocal tics—sudden involuntary movements or vocalizations. Tourette is known most for coprolalia (sudden yelling of obscenities), but this symptom is seen in only 25 to 30 percent of cases. Motor tics typically involve the head and neck. Vocal tics may be guttural sounds, repeated coughing, or words. Tourette was originally viewed as a psychological disorder, but in light of its responsiveness to medications, especially dopamine blockers, this view has changed. Although symptoms may be exacerbated by anxiety or tension, TS is now generally considered to be a neurological disorder that appears to involve dysfunction of dopaminergic pathways. TS is usually treated with dopamine (D2) blockers—haloperidol or pimozide, in low to moderate doses, or more recently, risperidone. Children with TS have a higher incidence of obsessive-compulsive disorder (OCD), attention-deficit/hyperactivity disorder (ADHD), and other learning disorders (Stern et al., 2000), probably because TS can involve multiple areas of the brain, some of which are also associated with OCD and ADHD. Theories regarding the etiology of TS include genetic (Robertson & Stern, 1997) and autoimmune mechanisms related to strep infection (Bowes, 2001).

Diagnostic Issues

The diagnosis of Tourette syndrome according to *DSM-IV-TR* (American Psychiatric Association, 2000) is based on the following criteria:

- Both motor and vocal tics have been present at some time during the illness, although not necessarily concurrently.

- The tics occur many times a day (usually in bouts) nearly every day for more than 1 year.

- The onset is before age 18.

Psychopharmacology

Using medication to reduce the intensity and frequency of tics may not be necessary and should not be considered an essential part of treatment. The goal of pharmacotherapy should be to suppress tics to a tolerable level, not to eliminate tics. Often, treatment of comorbid disorders, such as OCD or ADHD, is more important. When the tics are of sufficient severity that they are very embarrassing or interfere with other activities, pharmacological treatment should be considered. The mainstays of treatment for tic suppression are the dopamine blockers, such as haloperidol, pimozide, and fluphenazine. Haloperidol has been widely used, but pimozide and fluphenazine have fewer side effects. Although these medications are very effective in tic suppression, their neuroleptic side effects make them poorly tolerated. Although not approved by the FDA for treatment of TS, risperidone is now seen as a preferred treatment by some (Walkup, 2004). After adequate tic suppression is achieved, stimulants can be added for comorbid ADHD, or selective serotonin reuptake inhibitors (SSRIs) can be added for comorbid OCD. It is usually better to use the lowest dose sufficient to reduce tics rather than to use a higher dose to try to eliminate tics. These medications and their side effects are discussed in detail in chapter 5.

The alpha-adrenergic agonists clonidine and guanfacine represent another type of medication that has shown effectiveness. These medications were developed as antihypertensives and therefore may cause a severe drop in blood pressure. Because they also have some benefit in the treatment of ADHD, they may be most helpful in cases with comorbid ADHD, or when the dopamine blockers are not tolerated. Treatment with clonidine usually begins with 0.025 to 0.05 mg per day and increases slowly to 0.1 to 0.3 mg per day in 2 to 4 divided doses. Children should be monitored for sedation and low blood pressure. Guanfacine, though less studied, may cause less sedation, require less-frequent dosing, and have more impact on attention because of its preferential binding at prefrontal cortical regions and longer half-life.

CONDUCT DISORDER

The most important point we wish to make regarding conduct disorder (CD) is that the outward signs of aggression, antisocial behavior, and disregard for social rules that characterize conduct disorder are often seen in the context of other Axis I disorders. A common mistake is failure to diagnose an underlying and potentially treatable Axis I disorder. It is thus critical to conduct a comprehensive assessment to determine whether there is an underlying psychiatric disorder, especially one of the following: significant situational stress, bipolar disorder, major depression, ADHD, emotional dyscontrol secondary to neurological injury (seen in some children who have sustained closed head injuries, for example), and/or substance abuse. The only pharmacological treatments used for pure CD target aggression, irritability, and impulsivity. These medications include atypical antipsychotics (such as risperidone), clonidine, and SSRIs.

EATING DISORDERS

Eating disorders, which are fairly common in adolescents, can result in significant medical complications. There are three main types of eating disorders: anorexia nervosa, bulimia nervosa, and binge-eating disorder.

Anorexia involves the maintenance of a very low body weight by restriction of intake, purging, or both, often in combination with excessive exercising. Anorexia can be fatal, usually due to cardiac complications. Bulimia involves repeated episodes of bingeing and purging: eating large amounts of food and then purging through self-induced vomiting or use of laxatives or diuretics. It can lead to significant dental disease or gastrointestinal bleeding. Binge-eating disorder refers to consuming large amounts of food without purging. It leads to obesity.

Diagnostic Issues

For anorexia nervosa, the *DSM-IV-TR* diagnostic criteria are as follows:

- Body weight less than 85 percent of that expected

- Intense fear of gaining weight or becoming fat, despite being underweight

- Distortion of body image (perceiving oneself as overweight when actually underweight)

- Amenorrhea in postmenarcheal females (the absence of at least three consecutive menstrual cycles)

For bulimia nervosa, the *DSM-IV-TR* diagnostic criteria are as follows:

- Recurrent episodes of binge eating characterized by eating large amounts of food while feeling out of control

- Use of compensatory behavior to prevent weight gain, such as self-induced vomiting or misuse of laxatives or diuretics

- The binge eating and compensatory behaviors both occurring an average of at least twice a week for 3 months

Binge-eating disorder is subsumed under "Eating Disorder Not
Otherwise Specified" in *DSM-IV-TR* and is not an official separate disorder. The term refers to episodes of binge eating in the absence of compensatory behaviors to avoid gaining weight.

Psychopharmacology

Much research has investigated personality characteristics, psychological issues, family dynamics, and the biological basis of these
eating disorders. Anorexia usually requires a multimodal, if not multi-
disciplinary, treatment approach. The severe nutritional deficiency from
anorexia causes a multitude of problems that must be addressed medi-
cally and make response to medication treatment alone poor. Indeed,
no medication has shown significant consistent benefit in the treatment
of anorexia, with the possible exception of atypical antipsychotics. It is
known that endorphins are released during prolonged fasting, and one
theory suggests that patients with anorexia become addicted to starva-
tion, and that anorexics have a biological vulnerability to this addiction.
Studies have shown some benefit from naltrexone (an opiate antagonist)
in the treatment of anorexia—the explanation being that it blocks the
"high" of fasting and thereby removes the incentive (Luby, Marrazzi,
& Kinzie, 1987). Other medications that are *sometimes* helpful include
antidepressants, antipsychotics, cyproheptadine, lithium, and anticonvulsants. These drugs can be especially useful in cases with coexist-
ing features—antidepressants when depressive symptoms are present, for
example.

Patients with bulimia, in contrast, often benefit from treatment with
antidepressants (40 to 70 percent respond); this disorder is considered by
some to be a depressive variant. All types of antidepressants have proven
useful, although it should be remembered that bupropion (Wellbutrin) is
contraindicated in eating disorders because of increased risk of seizures.
SSRIs have been quite effective and, because of their low side-effect
profile, are the most widely used treatment.

The pharmacological treatment of binge-eating disorder is still under investigation, although there are reports that, like bulimia, it often responds to treatment with antidepressants or topiramate (Topamax).

SUBSTANCE ABUSE

Substance use has been shown to be common during adolescence, prompting widespread public concern. According to the CASA (National Center on Addiction and Substance Abuse) Report, in 2003 more than 40 percent of high schoolers admitted to drinking alcohol, and more than 20 percent admitted to having used marijuana in the past month (National Center on Addiction and Substance Abuse, 2004). The mainstay of the treatment of substance use and abuse disorders in adolescence, as in adults, continues to be nonpharmacological treatment, especially 12-step programs such as Alateen. However, medication can play an important role. It should, however, be noted that these medications have been studied almost exclusively in adults, so these suggestions are based on extrapolation from adult data and must be viewed with caution. Medications can help with the following:

- Treating intoxication (for example, naltrexone for heroin overdose)

- Treating withdrawal states (for example, benzodiazepines for alcohol withdrawal)

- Reducing craving

- Acting as a deterrent (for example, Antabuse)

- Treating comorbid psychiatric disorders

Diagnostic Issues

In the *DSM-IV-TR*, substance-related disorders are divided into the following categories: dependence, abuse, intoxication, and withdrawal. In addition, each substance may have related disorders phenomenologically similar to other disorders: delirium; dementia; and amnestic, psychotic, mood, anxiety, sexual, and sleep disorders.

Substance dependence is defined in the *DSM-IV-TR* as a pattern of substance use leading to significant impairment or distress, demonstrated by at least three of the following:

- Tolerance, as shown by either diminished effect with use of the same amount or a need for markedly increased amounts

- Withdrawal

- The substance often used more than was intended

- A persistent desire or unsuccessful efforts to cut down or control substance use

- A great deal of time spent obtaining the substance

- Giving up or reducing participation in important social, occupational, or recreational activities because of substance use

- Continued substance use despite having a problem that is likely to have been caused or exacerbated by the substance

DSM-IV-TR defines *substance abuse* as a pattern of substance use leading to significant impairment or distress, demonstrated by at least one of the following:

- Recurrent substance use resulting in a failure to fulfill obligations at work, school, or home

- Recurrent substance use in situations in which it is physically hazardous (for example, driving an automobile or operating a machine when impaired by substance use)

- Recurrent substance-related legal problems

- Continued substance use despite having persistent or recurrent social or interpersonal problems caused or exacerbated by the effects of the substance

Intoxication refers to an acutely altered mental state due to ingestion of, or exposure to, a substance.

Withdrawal refers to an altered state produced by cessation or reduction of use of a substance that causes significant impairment in functioning in important areas. The disorder may be "persisting"; in other words, it may continue even though substance use has stopped and the withdrawal syndrome has been resolved.

Substance	Dependence	Abuse	Intoxi-cation	With-drawal	Persisting
Alcohol	X	X	X	X	X
Hallucinogens	X	X	X		X
Opioids	X	X	X	X	
Phencyclidine	X	X	X		
Sedative-Hypnotics	X	X	X	X	X
Stimulants	X	X	X	X	X
Cannabis	X	X	X	X	
Figure 8-A					

MAJOR SUBSTANCE DIAGNOSES

Alcohol. Alcohol (ethanol) is a water-soluble substance that is rapidly absorbed and readily crosses the blood-brain barrier. It is a central nervous system (CNS) depressant and is metabolized by the liver, in addition to being a gastric irritant and toxic to liver cells and neurons. Alcohol is probably the most-studied substance of abuse (and the most abused substance). It is associated with dependence, abuse, withdrawal, intoxication, delirium, dementia, amnesia, delusions, hallucinations, mood disorder, anxiety disorder, sexual dysfunction, and sleep disorder. Much evidence demonstrates that alcoholism is familial, but the exact biological mechanism remains unclear.

Psychiatric symptoms are very common in alcohol intoxication and withdrawal, especially anxiety and depression. Often these symptoms will resolve within a few weeks without any pharmacological treatment. However, medications can play an important role in the treatment of alcohol-related disorders. Most of these medications are discussed elsewhere in this book, but a few are specific to alcoholism treatment. Disulfiram (Antabuse) is a medication used in abstinence maintenance. Disulfiram causes an accumulation of acetaldehyde if a person drinks alcohol while taking it, which leads to an unpleasant and potentially dangerous reaction involving flushing, throbbing headache, nausea, and vomiting. Only certain people are appropriate for disulfiram treatment. Some are able to remain abstinent without it; some will drink despite taking it. In between are those who will be able to reinforce their desire for abstinence by taking 125 to 500 mg of disulfiram once daily. Disulfiram should be used with caution because of its toxicity with alcohol and in overdose. It should only be used in the treatment of adolescents under close supervision. Two other medications have been shown to also help in abstinence maintenance by reducing craving: naltrexone, an opiate antagonist, has shown some promise (Bender, 1993), and acamprosate (Campral), a GABA receptor agonist, has been recently released to aid in abstinence maintenance. Acamprosate has been shown to be safe and well tolerated, but it does require dosing three times daily.

Stimulants. Amphetamines, ecstacy, and cocaine have become common substances of abuse. They are CNS stimulants that act on the dopaminergic system. Research suggests that a dopamine-mediated endogenous reward circuit in the limbic system is activated by amphetamines and cocaine. This means that use of these drugs is intensely pleasurable, hence their addictiveness.

Pharmacological treatment of stimulant use is different for each phase of use. During acute intoxication, medications such as benzodiazepines, beta-blockers, and clonidine can be used to block the acute effects of dopamine and norepinephrine (to control anxiety, heart rate, and blood pressure and prevent seizures). During withdrawal, medications such as antidepressants and amantadine are used to reduce craving (and hopefully subsequent use).

Opiates. Heroin was first synthesized from morphine over a century ago. Since then, it has become one of the most abused substances. Research into the reasons it produces such powerful effects has led to the discovery of specific opiate receptors and endogenous opioids (enkephalins and endorphins). These peptides appear to be neurotransmitters involved with the sensation of pain and pleasure. In clinical practice, the opiates are used primarily as analgesics. A number of the available opiates can lead to dependency, including morphine, heroin, propoxyphene (Darvon), methadone, meperidine (Demerol), pentazocine (Talwin), hydromorphone (Dilaudid), oxycodone (Percodan, Oxycontin), hydrocodone (Vicodin, Damason-P), and codeine.

Different medications are used to treat different phases of opiate use. Acute opiate intoxication leads to sedation, pupillary constriction, and respiratory depression and can be fatal. Specific antagonists, naloxone and naltrexone, block the opiate receptors and rapidly (and sometimes dramatically) reverse these effects. Opiate withdrawal is characterized by anxiety, agitation, sweating, gastrointestinal upset, tremulousness, and running nose. It is treated by using another opiate, such as propoxyphene (Darvon), methadone, or clonidine, or a combination of these. Dependence or abuse can be treated using one of two strategies. One is to administer methadone, a long-acting synthetic opiate that is well tolerated and reduces craving for other opiates such as heroin. Methadone is used for maintenance treatment because, with its long half-life, it produces less of a "high" and is less prone to abuse. The other is to use an opiate antagonist (naloxone, naltrexone, or buprenorphine) so the effect of the opiate will be blocked if it is used.

Hallucinogens. Various substances can produce transient psychotic states, often accompanied by visual, auditory, or olfactory hallucinations. These include LSD, mescaline, psilocybin, and PCP. These drugs are not associated with dependence or withdrawal, but they can produce florid psychosis during acute intoxication. This effect can be allowed to run its course (usually 12 to 24 hours), but sometimes medications, such as antianxiety or antipsychotic drugs, need to be used to decrease agitation and stabilize blood pressure. Severe overdoses of PCP can lead to convulsions and may require emergency medical treatment.

Marijuana and other drugs. Marijuana (cannabis) was not previously considered a drug that would produce tolerance, dependence, and abuse. However, possibly because current forms of marijuana may have ten times the THC (tetrahydrocannabinol) content of the marijuana of the 1970s, cannabis dependence, abuse, intoxication, delirium, psychotic disorder, mood disorder, and anxiety disorder are now recognized. Cannabis usually produces dependence because of its calming effect. Prolonged use leads to what has been called an "amotivational syndrome," associated with decreased initiative, activity, and energy. In some individuals, paradoxically, intoxication may lead to anxiety, and even psychosis. Withdrawal is usually associated with anxiety symptoms and occasionally paranoia. There are no specific treatments for cannabis-induced disorders. However, antianxiety medications are used for anxiety symptoms and antipsychotics are administered for psychotic symptoms.

Other substances of abuse, including nicotine, inhalants, and caffeine, are not covered here since their psychiatric effects are less important in a clinical setting.

APPENDIX

Patient and Caregiver Information Sheets on Psychiatric Medications

PATIENT AND CAREGIVER INFORMATION ON ANTIDEPRESSANTS

The name of your medication is: _____ .

IMPORTANT NOTE: The following information is intended to supplement, not substitute for, the expertise and judgment of your physician, pharmacist, or other health care professional. It is not intended to imply that use of the drug is safe, appropriate, or effective for you. This information contains limited and general information about these medications, and it is not all-inclusive. Not all uses, side effects, precautions, or drug interactions are listed. Your doctor or pharmacist will provide you with official patient information that is more complete and detailed. Consult your health care professional before using this drug.

Uses

SSRI antidepressants and other more recently developed antidepressants such as Effexor, Remeron, and Cymbalta are used in the treatment of a number of disorders, including major depressive disorder, depression associated with manic depressive illness (bipolar disorder), obsessive-compulsive disorder, panic disorder, generalized anxiety disorder, eating disorders, social phobia, post-traumatic stress disorder, and premenstrual changes in mood. The antidepressant Wellbutrin is an effective antidepressant, but is generally not used to treat anxiety or eating disorders. These drugs have also been found to be effective in the treatment of several other disorders, including mild depression, separation anxiety disorder, and impulsive or aggressive behavior, although they are not currently approved for these indications.

The doctor may choose to prescribe this medication for a reason not listed here. If you are not sure why this medication is being prescribed, please ask the doctor.

How To Use

Take as directed, usually once a day by mouth. Some side effects, such as nausea, may be reduced by taking the medication with food. It is best to take it at about the same time each day. The dosage is based on your medical condition and response to therapy.

MISSED DOSE

If you miss a dose, take it as soon as you remember. However, if it is near the time of the next dose, or the next day, skip the missed dose and resume your usual dosing schedule. *Do not double the dose in order to catch up.*

Side Effects

Side effects occur, to some degree, with all medications. They are usually not serious and do not occur in all individuals. They may sometimes occur before beneficial effects of the medication are noticed. Most side effects will decrease or disappear with time. If a side effect persists, speak to the doctor about appropriate treatment.

Common side effects that should be reported to the doctor at the next appointment include drowsiness and fatigue; anxiety or nervousness, including problems sleeping; headache; nausea or heartburn; muscle tremor; twitching; changes in sex drive or sexual performance; blurred vision; dry mouth; nightmares; and loss of appetite.

Tell your doctor immediately if any of the following unlikely but serious side effects occurs: soreness of the mouth, gums, or throat; skin rash or itching; swelling of the face; any unusual bruising or bleeding; nausea; vomiting; loss of appetite; fatigue; weakness; fever or flu-like symptoms; yellow tinge of the eyes or skin; dark-colored urine; inability to pass urine; tingling in the hands and feet; severe muscle twitching; severe agitation or restlessness; *a switch in mood to an unusual state of happiness, excitement, or irritability, or a marked disturbance in sleep*; or thoughts of suicide or hostility (in rare instances this medication has been associated with some suicidal or hostile thoughts; although these thoughts may be seen as a part of the disorder, you should definitely discuss these kinds of thoughts with your doctor).

Report any other side effects not listed above to your physician.

Drug Interactions

Because SSRI antidepressant drugs can change the effects of other medication or may be affected by other medication, always check with the doctor or pharmacist before taking any other drugs, including over-the-counter medications such as cold remedies. Inform all doctors and dentists who examine or treat you that you are taking an antidepressant drug.

PRECAUTIONS

- Before taking this medication, tell your doctor or pharmacist if you are allergic to it (if known) or if you have any other allergies.

- Do not increase or decrease your dose without consulting your doctor.

- This drug may make you dizzy or drowsy; use caution engaging in activities requiring alertness, such as riding a bike, driving, or using machinery.

- Avoid alcoholic beverages.

- Avoid excessive amounts of caffeine.

- Do not stop your drug suddenly, as this may result in withdrawal symptoms such as muscle aches, chills, tingling in your hands or feet, nausea, vomiting, and dizziness.

- All antidepressants can increase the likelihood of seizures. Because of this risk, bupropion (Wellbutrin), in particular, should not be used by persons with bulimia.

- *If you have any questions regarding this medication, do not hesitate to contact the doctor, pharmacist, or nurse.*

PATIENT AND CAREGIVER INFORMATION ON ANTIANXIETY MEDICATIONS

The name of your medication is: _____ .

IMPORTANT NOTE: The following information is intended to supplement, not substitute for, the expertise and judgment of your physician, pharmacist, or other health care professional. It is not intended to imply that use of the drug is safe, appropriate, or effective for you. This information contains limited and general information about these medications, and it is not all-inclusive. Not all uses, side effects, precautions, or drug interactions are listed. Your doctor or pharmacist will provide you with official patient information that is more complete and detailed. Consult your health care professional before using this drug.

Uses

Antianxiety medications can help relieve the symptoms of anxiety but will not alter its cause. In usually prescribed doses, they help to calm and sedate the individual; in higher doses these drugs may be used to induce sleep. These medications, known as benzodiazepines, may also be used as a muscle relaxant, to treat agitation, to suppress seizures, and prior to some diagnostic procedures or surgery.

The doctor may choose to use this medication for a reason not listed here. If you are not sure why this medication is being prescribed, please ask the doctor.

How To Use

Anxiolytic drugs can reduce agitation and induce calm or sedation usually within an hour. Depending on the medication, they may be taken up to three or four times per day.

MISSED DOSE

Often this type of medication is taken on a PRN, or as needed, basis. However, if you have been instructed to take the medication on a regular basis, you may wait until the next scheduled time if you miss a dose. *Do not double the dose in order to catch up.*

Side Effects

Side effects occur, to some degree, with all medications. They are usually not serious and do not occur in all individuals. They may sometimes occur before beneficial effects of the medication are noticed. Most side effects will decrease or disappear with time. If a side effect persists, speak to the doctor about appropriate treatment.

Common side effects that should be reported to the doctor at the next appointment include drowsiness and fatigue, loss of coordination, weakness or dizziness, forgetfulness, memory lapses, slurred speech, nausea, and heartburn.

Tell your doctor immediately if any of the following unlikely but serious side effects occurs: disorientation; confusion; worsening of memory; difficulty learning new things; blackouts; amnesia; nervousness, restlessness, excitement, or any other behavior changes; loss of coordination leading to falls; or skin rash.

This type of medication may impair the mental and physical abilities required for driving a car or riding a bike. Avoid these activities if you feel drowsy or slowed down.

Do not stop taking the drug suddenly, especially if you have been on the medication for a number of months or have been taking high doses. Benzodiazepines need to be reduced gradually in order to prevent withdrawal reactions.

Report any other side effects not listed above to your physician.

Drug Interactions

Because antianxiety medications may be affected by other medication, always check with the doctor or pharmacist before taking any other drugs, including over-the-counter medication such as cold remedies, especially those that are sedating. Inform all doctors and dentists who examine or treat you that you are taking an antianxiety medication.

PRECAUTIONS

- Before taking this medication, tell your doctor or pharmacist if you are allergic to it (if known) or if you have any other allergies.

- Do not increase or decrease your dose without consulting your doctor.

- *If you have any questions regarding this medication, do not hesitate to contact the doctor, pharmacist, or nurse.*

PATIENT AND CAREGIVER INFORMATION ON ANTICONVULSANT MOOD STABILIZERS

The name of your medication is: _____.

IMPORTANT NOTE: The following information is intended to supplement, not substitute for, the expertise and judgment of your physician, pharmacist, or other health care professional. It is not intended to imply that use of the drug is safe, appropriate, or effective for you. This information contains limited and general information about these medications, and it is not all-inclusive. Not all uses, side effects, precautions, or drug interactions are listed. Your doctor or pharmacist will provide you with official patient information that is more complete and detailed. Consult your health care professional before using this drug.

Common Drug Names

(Brand and generic)

Depakote   (divalproex)

Depakene   (valproic acid)

Tegretol, Equetro   (carbamazepine)

Uses

These medications can be used to treat bipolar disorder, but they are primarily used to treat seizure disorders.

How To Use

A variety of products are available in different strengths; some are short acting and some are long acting. A lower starting dose is prescribed, followed by slowly increasing dosages. Your doctor will determine the best dosing schedule for you. You will need to have regular blood tests to check the amount of medication in your system. After the medication is started, some improvement may be noted within the first week, followed by continued lessening of symptoms over the next several weeks or months. Treatment with the medication is considered long term.

MISSED DOSE

If you miss a dose, take it as soon as you remember. However, if it is near the time of the next dose, or the next day, skip the missed dose and resume your usual dosing schedule. *Do not double the dose in order to catch up.*

Side Effects

Side effects occur, to some degree, with all medications. They are usually not serious and do not occur in all individuals. They may sometimes occur before beneficial effects of the medication are noticed. Most side effects will decrease or disappear with time. If a side effect persists, speak to the doctor about appropriate treatment.

You should seek immediate medical attention if you experience rash, blistering, or crusting of the skin; itching; swelling; difficulty breathing; mouth sores; lethargy; weakness; confusion; blurred vision; unusual eye movements; lack of coordination; tremor; fever or flu-like symptoms; unusual bruising; bleeding or skin blotching; yellow discoloration of the skin or yellow tinge in the eyes; nausea; vomiting; extreme loss of appetite; difficulty urinating; or dark-colored urine.

Although rare, severe liver problems may occur with these medications. Contact your doctor immediately if you experience vomiting, unusual tiredness, or swelling of the face.

A rare and serious side effect of divalproex is pancreatitis. Tell your doctor immediately if you develop stomach pain, nausea, vomiting, or loss of appetite.

Common side effects that should be reported to the doctor as soon as possible include drowsiness, dizziness, dry mouth, nausea, hair loss (valproate), changes in the menstrual cycle (valproate), and weight change.

Report any other side effects not listed above to your physician.

Drug Interactions

Check with the doctor or pharmacist before starting, stopping, or changing the dose of any other medicines, including over-the-counter and herbal products.

Certain antibiotics may cause carbamazepine levels to increase. Carbamazepine may cause birth controls pills to be less effective.

PRECAUTIONS

- Before taking this medication, tell your doctor or pharmacist if you are allergic to it (if known) or if you have any other allergies.

- Take exactly as prescribed. Do not increase your dose unless instructed by your doctor. Taking too much medication can result in serious side effects.

- Follow your doctor's instructions regarding getting your blood levels checked.

- Do not chew or crush the tablets or capsules unless directed to do so by your doctor or pharmacist.

- Take with food or milk to prevent stomach upset.

- This medicine may cause fatigue, light-headedness, or blurred vision. Use caution when operating machinery, driving, or performing tasks that require alertness or clear vision.

- Carbamazepine may cause increased sensitivity to sunlight.

- Do not stop taking your medication suddenly unless told to do so by your doctor. Abruptly stopping the medicine may cause your bipolar symptoms to return.

- Make sure that your doctor knows about all your medical conditions.

- Inform your doctor or pharmacist about all other medicines you are taking, including over-the-counter products.

- Avoid drinking grapefruit juice while taking carbamazepine, since it can affect the level of carbamazepine in your body.

- Do not drink alcohol while taking this medication.

- Tell your doctor if the medicine does not seem to be working or if your condition gets worse.

- Consult with your doctor if you think you might be pregnant.

- Check with your doctor before breastfeeding.

- *If you have any questions regarding this medication, do not hesitate to contact the doctor, pharmacist, or nurse.*

PATIENT AND CAREGIVER INFORMATION ON LITHIUM

The name of your medication is: _____.

IMPORTANT NOTE: The following information is intended to supplement, not substitute for, the expertise and judgment of your physician, pharmacist, or other health care professional. It is not intended to imply that use of the drug is safe, appropriate, or effective for you. This information contains limited and general information about these medications, and it is not all-inclusive. Not all uses, side effects, precautions, or drug interactions are listed. Your doctor or pharmacist will provide you with official patient information that is more complete and detailed. Consult your health care professional before using this drug.

Common Brand Names

Eskalith, Lithonate, Lithobid

Use

Lithium is primarily used to treat bipolar disorder.

How To Use

A variety of products are available in different strengths; some are short acting and some are long acting. A lower starting dose is prescribed followed by slowly increasing dosages. Your doctor will determine the best dosing schedule for you. You will need to have regular blood tests to check the amount of lithium in your system. After the medication is started, some improvement may be noted within the first week, followed by continued lessening of symptoms over the next several weeks or months. Treatment with the medication is considered long term.

MISSED DOSE

If you miss a dose, take it as soon as you remember. However, if it is near the time of the next dose, or the next day, skip the missed dose and resume your usual dosing schedule. *Do not double the dose in order to catch up.*

Side Effects

Side effects occur, to some degree, with all medications. They are usually not serious and do not occur in all individuals. They may sometimes occur before beneficial effects of the medication are noticed. Most side effects will decrease or disappear with time. If a side effect persists, speak to the doctor about appropriate treatment.

Although rare, rash, itching, swelling, or difficulty breathing sometimes occurs with lithium. Contact your doctor immediately if you experience vomiting, unusual tiredness, or swelling of the face while taking lithium.

Some side effects might mean that you have too much lithium in your system which could be very serious. You should report the following side effects to the doctor *immediately*: clumsiness, loss of balance, feeling of intoxication, slurred speech, double vision, vomiting or diarrhea, tremors or shakiness of the hands, and change in mood or behavior.

Common side effects that should be reported to the doctor as soon as possible include difficulty concentrating, mild nausea, weight change, increased thirst and urination, and acne or skin problems.

Report any other side effects not listed above to your physician.

Drug Interactions

Check with the doctor or pharmacist before starting, stopping, or changing the dose of any other medicines, including over-the-counter and herbal products.

Potentially serious drug interactions can occur with diuretic medications (water pills) and nonsteroidal anti-inflammatory medications by causing lithium levels to rise.

PRECAUTIONS

* Before taking this medication, tell your doctor or pharmacist if you are allergic to it (if known) or if you have any other allergies.

117

- Take exactly as prescribed. Do not increase your dose unless instructed by your doctor. Taking too much lithium can result in serious side effects.

- Follow your doctor's instructions regarding getting your blood levels checked.

- Do not chew or crush the tablets or capsules unless directed to do so by your doctor or pharmacist.

- Take with food or milk to prevent stomach upset.

- Drink 8 to 12 glasses of water or fluid every day.

- Maintain your normal diet and do not change the amount of salt in your diet unless instructed by your doctor.

- Limit caffeine intake.

- This medicine may cause fatigue, light-headedness, or blurred vision. Use caution when operating machinery, driving, or performing tasks that require alertness or clear vision.

- Do not stop taking your medication suddenly unless told to do so by your doctor. Abruptly stopping the medicine may cause your bipolar symptoms to return.

- Make sure that your doctor knows about all your medical conditions.

- If you become sick with any flu-like virus or have a fever, check with your doctor to see if any changes in your lithium dose are necessary.

- Be careful not to become dehydrated when exercising, during hot weather, or any time you sweat excessively (for example, in saunas and hot tubs). Losing water and salt from your body may cause your blood lithium level to increase.

- Inform your doctor or pharmacist about all other medicines you are taking, including over-the-counter products.

- Do not drink alcohol while taking this medication.

- Tell your doctor if the medicine does not seem to be working or if your condition gets worse.

- Consult with your doctor if you think you might be pregnant.

- Check with your doctor before breastfeeding.

- *If you have any questions regarding this medication, do not hesitate to contact the doctor, pharmacist, or nurse.*

PATIENT AND CAREGIVER INFORMATION ON PSYCHOSTIMULANTS

The name of your medication is: _____.

IMPORTANT NOTE: The following information is intended to supplement, not substitute for, the expertise and judgment of your physician, pharmacist, or other health care professional. It is not intended to imply that use of the drug is safe, appropriate, or effective for you. This information contains limited and general information about these medications, and it is not all-inclusive. Not all uses, side effects, precautions, or drug interactions are listed. Your doctor or pharmacist will provide you with official patient information that is more complete and detailed. Consult your health care professional before using this drug.

Uses

Psychostimulants are used primarily in the treatment of attention-deficit/hyperactivity disorder (ADHD) in children and adults. These drugs are also approved for use in the treatment of narcolepsy.

Although they are not currently approved for this indication, psychostimulants have been found useful in the treatment of refractory depression.

The doctor may choose to use this medication for a reason not listed here. If you are not sure why this medication is being prescribed, please ask the doctor.

How To Use

Take as directed, usually starting in the morning up to three times per day by mouth. Some side effects may be reduced by taking the medication with food. It is best to take it at about the same time each day. The dosage is based on your medical condition and response to therapy.

MISSED DOSE

If you miss a dose, take it as soon as you remember. However, if it is near the time of the next dose, or the next day, skip the missed dose and resume your usual dosing schedule. *Do not double the dose in order to catch up.*

Side Effects

Side effects occur, to some degree, with all medications. They are usually not serious and do not occur in all individuals. They may sometimes occur before beneficial effects of the medication are noticed. Most side effects will decrease or disappear with time. If a side effect persists, speak to the doctor about appropriate treatment.

Common side effects that should be reported to the doctor at the next appointment include difficulty sleeping, nervousness, excitability, loss of appetite, weight loss, increased heart rate and blood pressure, headache, nausea or heartburn, dry mouth, and dizziness.

Tell your doctor immediately if any of the following unlikely but serious side effects occurs: muscle twitches or tics; fast or irregular heartbeat; persistent throbbing headache; soreness of mouth, gums, or throat; rash; unusual bruising or bleeding; nausea and vomiting; yellow tinge of eyes or skin; severe agitation or restlessness; *a switch in mood to an unusual state of happiness or irritability; or other fluctuations in mood.*

Report any other side effects not listed above to your physician.

Drug Interactions

Because psychostimulants can change the effects of other medication, or may be affected by other medication, always check with the doctor or pharmacist before taking other drugs, including over-the-counter medication such as cold remedies. Inform all doctors and dentists who treat or examine you that you are taking a psychostimulant drug.

PRECAUTIONS

- Before taking this medication, tell your doctor or pharmacist if you are allergic to it (if known) or if you have any other allergies.

- Do not increase or decrease your dose without consulting your doctor.

- *If you have any questions regarding this medication, do not hesitate to contact the doctor, pharmacist, or nurse.*

PATIENT AND CAREGIVER INFORMATION ON ANTIPSYCHOTICS

The name of your medication is: _____ .

IMPORTANT NOTE: The following information is intended to supplement, not substitute for, the expertise and judgment of your physician, pharmacist, or other health care professional. It is not intended to imply that use of the drug is safe, appropriate, or effective for you. This information contains limited and general information about these medications, and it is not all-inclusive. Not all uses, side effects, precautions, or drug interactions are listed. Your doctor or pharmacist will provide you with official patient information that is more complete and detailed. Consult your health care professional before using this drug.

Uses

This medication is used to treat certain mental/mood conditions, such as schizophrenia and bipolar mania. It works by helping to restore the balance of certain natural chemicals in the brain (neurotransmitters). Some of the benefits of continued use of this medication include reduced nervousness, better concentration, and reduced episodes of confusion.

How To Use

Take as directed, usually once a day by mouth with or without food. Stand up slowly, especially when starting this medication, to avoid dizziness. The dosage is based on your medical condition and response to therapy. Use this medication regularly in order to get the most benefit from it. Remember to use it at the same time each day.

Missed Dose

If you miss a dose, take it as soon as you remember. However, if it is near the time of the next dose, or the next day, skip the missed dose and resume your usual dosing schedule. *Do not double the dose in order to catch up.*

Side Effects

Side effects occur, to some degree, with all medications. They are usually not serious and do not occur in all individuals. They may sometimes occur before beneficial effects of the medication are noticed. Most side effects will decrease or disappear with time. If a side effect persists, speak to the doctor about appropriate treatment.

Common side effects that should be reported to the doctor at the next appointment include dizziness, stomach pain, dry mouth, constipation, weight gain, and drowsiness. If any of these effects persists or worsens, notify your doctor or pharmacist promptly.

To minimize dizziness or fainting, stand up slowly when rising from a seated or lying position, especially when you first start using this medication.

Tell your doctor immediately if any of the following unlikely but serious side effects occurs: fast heartbeat, ankle or leg swelling, agitation, confusion, restlessness, weakness, difficulty speaking, numbness or tingling of hands or feet, trouble walking (abnormal gait), painful menstrual periods, pink urine, tremor, muscle spasm or rigidity, chest pain, yellowing of the eyes or skin, one-sided weakness, sudden vision changes or other eye problems, headache, painful urination, seizures, or difficulty swallowing.

This drug infrequently causes blood sugar levels to rise, which can cause or worsen diabetes. High blood sugar can, in rare cases, cause serious (sometimes fatal) conditions such as diabetic coma. Tell your doctor immediately if you develop symptoms of high blood sugar, such as unusual increased thirst and urination. If you already have diabetes, be sure to check your blood sugar levels regularly.

This drug may also cause significant weight gain and a rise in your blood cholesterol (or triglyceride) levels. These effects, along with diabetes, may increase your risk for developing heart disease. Discuss the risks and benefits of treatment with your doctor.

This medication can in rare cases cause a serious condition called neuroleptic malignant syndrome (NMS). Tell your doctor immediately if you develop any of the following symptoms: fever, muscle stiffness, severe confusion, sweating, or fast or irregular heartbeat.

In rare cases antipsychotics cause a condition known as tardive dyskinesia. In some cases, this condition may be permanent. Tell your doctor immediately if you develop any unusual or uncontrolled movements (especially of the face or tongue).

Report any other side effects not listed above to your physician.

Drug Interactions

Before using this medication, tell your doctor or pharmacist about all prescription medications and over-the-counter or herbal products you are using, especially carbamazepine, fluvoxamine, omeprazole, rifampin, drugs for high blood pressure, and drugs for Parkinson's disease.

Report drugs that cause drowsiness, because this effect will be increased by taking them in combination with this medication.

Do not start or stop any medicine without doctor or pharmacist approval.

PRECAUTIONS

- Before taking this medication, tell your doctor or pharmacist if you are allergic to it (if known) or if you have any other allergies.

- Do not increase or decrease your dose without consulting your doctor.

- This drug may make you dizzy or drowsy; use caution when engaging in activities requiring alertness, such as riding a bike, driving, or using machinery.

- Avoid alcoholic beverages.

- Avoid excessive amounts of caffeine.

- This medication can make you prone to heat stroke. Avoid activities that might cause you to overheat (such as doing strenuous work, exercising in hot weather, and using hot tubs).

- Do not share this medication with others.

- Laboratory and/or medical tests (such as fasting blood sugar, weight, blood pressure, blood cholesterol/triglyceride levels, and liver function tests) should be performed periodically to monitor your progress and check for side effects. Consult your doctor for more details.

- Go for regular eye exams as part of your regular health care regimen, and to check for any unlikely, but possible, eye problems.

- *If you have any questions regarding this medication, do not hesitate to contact the doctor, pharmacist, or nurse.*

References

American Diabetes Association, American Psychiatric Association, & the American Association of Clinical Endocrinologists. (2004). Consensus development conference on antipsychotic drugs and obesity and diabetes. *Journal of Clinical Psychiatry, 65,* 267–272.

American Psychiatric Association. (1987). *Diagnostic and statistical manual of mental disorders* (3rd ed., Rev. ed.). Washington, DC.

American Psychiatric Association. (2000). *Diagnostic and statistical manual of mental disorders* (4th ed., Text revision). Washington, DC.

Asperger, H. (1991). Die autistischen psychopathen im kindesalter. In *Autism and Asperger Syndrome* (pp. 37–92). (U. Frith, Trans.). Cambridge, England: Cambridge University Press. (Original work published 1944).

Ballenger, J. C., & Post, R. M. (1980). Carbamazepine in manic-depressive illness: A new treatment. *American Journal of Psychiatry, 137,* 782–790.

Barkley, R. A. (2000). *Taking charge of ADHD.* New York: Guilford Press.

Barnhart, W. J., Makela, E. H., & Latocha, M. J. (2004). SSRI-induced apathy syndrome: A clinical review. *Journal of Psychiatric Practice, 10*(3), 196–199.

Baron-Cohen, S., Leslie, A., & Frith, U. (1985). Does the autistic child have a "theory of mind"? *Cognition, 21,* 37–46.

Baron-Cohen, S., Jolliffe, T., Mortimore, C., & Robertson, M. (1997). Another advanced test of theory of mind: Evidence from very high functioning adults with Autism or Asperger syndrome. *Journal of Child Psychological Psychiatry, 38,* 813–822.

Baxter, L. R. (1991). PET studies of cerebral function in major depression and obsessive-compulsive disorder: The emerging prefrontal cortex consensus. *Annals of Clinical Psychiatry, 3,* 103–109.

Baxter, L. R., Schwartz, J. M., Bergman, K. S., Szuba, M. P., Guze, B. H., Marriotta, J. C., et al. (1992). Caudate glucose metabolic rate changes with both drug and behavior therapy for obsessive-compulsive disorder. *Archives of General Psychiatry, 49,* 681–689.

Bender, K. J. (Ed.). (1993). Narcotic antagonist for alcoholism. *Psychotropics, 13,* 6–8.

Bertolino, A., Frye, M., Callicott, J. H., Mattay, V. S., Rakow, R., Shelton-Repella, J., et al. (2003). Neuronal pathology in the hippocampal area of patients with bipolar disorder: A study with proton magnetic resonance spectroscopic imaging. *Biological Psychiatry, 53,* 906–913.

Bhalla, U. S., & Iyengar, R. (1999). Emergent properties of networks of biological signaling pathways. *Science, 283,* 381–387.

Biederman, J., Birmaher, B., & Carlson, G. (2000). Roundtable on prepubertal bipolar disorder. Retrieved January 1, 2005, from www.nimh.nih.gov/dmdba/prepubertal.dvm.

Biederman, J., Hirshfeld-Becker, D. R., Rosenbaum, J. F., Herot, C., Friedman, D., Snidman, N., et al. (2001). Further evidence of association between behavioral inhibition and social anxiety in children. *American Journal of Psychiatry, 158,* 1673–1679.

Biederman, J., Mick, E., Faraone, S. V., Spencer, T., Wilens, T. E., & Wozniak, J. (2003). Current concepts in the validity, diagnosis, and treatment of pediatric bipolar disorder. *International Journal of Neuropsychopharmacology, 6,* 293–300.

Biederman, J., Wilens, T., Mick, E., Spencer, T., & Faraone, S. V. (1999). Pharmacotherapy for attention-deficit/hyperactivity disorder reduces risk for substance abuse disorder. *Pediatrics, 104*(2), e20.

Biederman, J, Birmaher, B., Carlson, G. A., Chang, K. D., Fenton, W. S., Geller, B., et al. (2001). National Institute of Mental Health research roundtable on prepubertal bipolar disorder. *Journal of the American Academy of Child and Adolescent Psychiatry, 40,* 871–878.

Birmaher, B., Kennah, H., Brent, D., Ehmann, M., Bridge, J., & Axelson, D. (2002). Is bipolar disorder specifically associated with panic disorder in youths? *Journal of Clinical Psychiatry, 63*(5), 414–419.

Bowes, M. (2001). OCD: Will immunotherapy succeed where other approaches have failed? *Neuropsychiatry Reviews, 2,* 1–25.

Brotman, A. (1992). *Practical reviews in psychiatry.* Birmingham, AL: Educational Reviews.

Brown University. (2004). Experts, parents weigh in at FDA's public hearing on SSRI safety. *Child and Adolescent Psychopharmacology Update, 6*(3), 1–3.

Campbell, M., Anderson, L. T., Small, A. M., Adams, P., Gonzalez, N. M., & Ernst, M. (1993). Naltrexone in autistic children: behavioral symptoms and attentional learning. *Journal of the American Academy of Child and Adolescent Psychiatry, 32,* 1283–1291.

Carlson, G. A., Bromet, E. J., & Sievers, S. (2000). Phenomenology and outcome of subjects with early- and adult-onset psychotic mania. *American Journal of Psychiatry, 157*(2), 213–219.

Carlson, G. A., Jensen, P. S, Findling, R. L., Meyer, R. E., Calabrese, J., DelBello, M. P., et al. (2003). Methodological issues and controversies in clinical trials with child and adolescent patients with bipolar disorder: Report of a consensus conference. *Journal of Child and Adolescent Psychopharmacology, 13*(1), 13–27.

Castellanos, F. X., Lee, P. P., Sharp, W., Jeffries, N. O., Greenstein, D. K., Clasen, L. S., et al. (2002). Developmental trajectories of brain volume abnormalities in children and adolescents with attention-deficit/hyperactivity disorder. *Journal of the American Medical Association, 288*(14), 1740–1748.

Chang, K., Adleman, N., Dienes, K., Barnea-Goraly, N., Reiss, A., & Ketter, T. (2003, June 1). Decreased N-acetylaspartate in children with familial bipolar disorder. *Biological Psychiatry, 53*(11), 1059–1065.

Chen, H. H., Nicoletti, M. A., Hatch, J. P., Sassi, R. B., Axelson, D., Brambilla, P., et al. (2004, June 3). Abnormal left superior temporal gyrus volumes in children and adolescents with bipolar disorder: A magnetic resonance imaging study. *Neuroscience Letters, 363*(1),65–68.

Cohen, I., Tsiouris, J. A., & Pfadt, A. (1991). Effects of long-acting propranolol on agonistic and stereotyped behaviors in a man with pervasive developmental disorder and fragile-X syndrome: A double-blind, placebo-controlled study. *Journal of Clinical Psychopharmacology, 11,* 398–399.

Conners, C. K., & Barkley, R.A. (1985). Rating scales and checklists for child psychopharmacology. *Psychopharmacology Bulletin, 21,* 809–851.

Cook, E. H., Wagner, K. D., March, J. S., Biederman, J., Landau, P., Wolkow, R., et al. (2001). Long-term sertraline treatment of children and adolescents with obsessive-compulsive disorder. *Journal of Child and Adolescent Psychopharmacology, 40,* 1175–1181.

Costello, E. J., Pine, D. S., Hammen, C., March, J. S., Plotsky, P. M., Weissman, M. M., et al. (2002). Development and natural history of mood disorders. *Biological Psychiatry, 52,* 529–542.

Coyle, J. T., Pine, D. S., Charney, D. S., Lewis, L., Nemeroff, C. F., Carlson, G. A., et al. (2003). Depression and bipolar support alliance consensus statement on the unmet needs in diagnosis and treatment of mood disorders in children and adolescents. *Journal of the American Academy of Child and Adolescent Psychiatry, 42,* 12.

Deckersbach, T., Otto, M. W., Savage, C. R., Baer, L., & Jenike, M. A. (2000). The relationship between semantic organization and memory in obsessive-compulsive disorder. *Psychotherapy and Psychosomatics, 69,* 101–107.

Emslie, G. J., & Mayes, T. C. (2001). Mood disorders in children and adolescents: Psychopharmacological treatment. *Biological Psychiatry, 49,* 1082–1090.

Findling, R. L., McNamara, N. K., Gracious, B. L., Youngstrom, E. A., Stansbrey, R. J., Reed, M. D., et al. (2003). Combination lithium and divalproex sodium in pediatric bipolarity. *Journal of the American Academy of Child and Adolescent Psychiatry, 42,* 895–901.

Fombonne, E. (2005). Epidemiology of autistic disorder and other pervasive developmental disorders. *Journal of Clinical Psychiatry, 66*(Suppl. 10), 3–8.

Geller, B., Craney, J. L., Bolhofner, K., Nickelsburg, M. J., Williams, M., & Zimerman, B. (2002). Two-year prospective follow-up of children with a prepubertal and early adolescent bipolar disorder phenotype. *American Journal of Psychiatry, 159,* 927–933.

Geller, B., & DelBello, M. P. (Eds.) (2003). *Bipolar disorder in childhood and early adolescence.* New York: Guilford Press.

Geller, B., Sun, K., Luby, J., Frazier, J., & Williams, M. (1995). Complex and rapid-cycling in bipolar children and adolescents: A preliminary study. *Journal of Affective Disorders, 34,* 259–268.

Glass, R. M. (2004). Treatment of adolescents with major depression: Contributions of a major trial. *Journal of the American Medical Association, 292*(7), 861–863.

Goodwin, F. K., & Jamison, K. R. (2007). *Manic-depressive illness,* second edition. Oxford, England: Oxford University Press.

Gorman, J., Kent, J. M., Sullivan, G. M., & Coplan, J. D. (2000). Neuroanatomical hypthesis of panic disorder, revised. *American Journal of Psychiatry, 157,* 493–505.

Greenhill, L. L., Abikoff, H. B., Arnold, L. E., Cantwell, D. P., Conners, C. K., Elliott, G., et al. (1996). Medication treatment strategies in the MTA study: Relevance to clinicians and researchers. *Journal* of the American Academy of Child and Adolescent Psychiatry, 35, 1304–1313.

Hechtman, L., & Greenfield, B. (2003). Long-term use of stimulants in children with attention hyperactivity disorder: Safety, efficacy, and long-term outcome. *Paediatric Drugs* (New Zealand), 5(12), 787–794.

Hviid, A., Stellfeld, M., Wohlfahrt, J., & Melbye, M. (2003). Association between thimerosal-containing vaccine and autism. *Journal of the American Medical Association, 290*(13), 1763–1766.

Jureidini, J., Doecke, C. J., Mansfield, P. R., Haby, M. M., Menkes, D. B., & Tonkin, A. L. (2004). Efficacy and safety of antidepressants for children and adolescents. *British Medical Journal, 328,* 879–883.

Kagan, J. (1998). *Galens's prophecy: Temperament in human nature.* New York: Basic Books.

Kanner, L. (1943). Autistic disturbances of affective contact. *Nervous Diseases in Children, 2,* 217–250.

Keck, P., McElroy, S., Strakowski, S., West, S., Sax, K., Hawkins, J., et al. (1998). 12-month outcome of patients with bipolar disorder following hospitalization for a manic or mixed episode. *American Journal of Psychiatry, 155,* 646–652.

Kelsoe, J. R., Spence, M. A., Loetscher, E., Foguet, M., Sadovnick, A. D., Remick, R. A., et al. (2001). A genome survey indicates a possible susceptibility locus for bipolar disorder on chromosome 22. *Proceedings of the National Academy of Science USA, 98,* 585–590.

Kerr, A. M., Armstrong, D. D., Prescott, R. J., Doyle, D., & Kearney, D. L. (1997). Rett syndrome: Analysis of death in the British survey. *European Child and Adolescent Psychiatry 6*(Suppl.), 71–74.

Kolmen, B. K., Feldman, H. M., Handen, B. L., & Janosky, J. E. (1995). Naltrexone in young autistic children: A double-blind placebo-controlled crossover study. *Journal of the American Academy of Child and Adolescent Psychiatry, 34,* 223–231.

Kowatch, R. A., Fristad, M., Birmaher, B., Wagner, K., Findling, R., & Hellander, M. (2005). Treatment guidelines for children and adolescents with bipolar disorder. *Journal of the American Academy of Child and Adolescent Psychiatry, 44,* 213–235.

Kowatch, R. A., Suppes, T., Carmody, T. J., Bucci, J. P., Hume, J. H., Kromelis, M., et al. (2000). Effect size of lithium, divalproex sodium, and carbamazepine in children and adolescents with bipolar disorder. *Journal of the American Academy of Child and Adolescent Psychiatry, 39,* 713–720.

Kuczenski, R., & Segal, D. S. (2002). Exposure of adolescent rats to oral methylphenidate. *Journal of Neuroscience, 22,* 264–271.

Kumra, S. (2000). The diagnosis and treatment of children and adolescents with schizophrenia; "My mind is playing tricks on me." *Child and Adolescent Psychiatric Clinics of North America, 9,* 183–197.

Lewinsohn, P. M., Klein, D. N., & Seeley, J. R. (1995). Bipolar disorders in a community sample of older adolescents: Prevalence, phenomenology, comorbidity, and course. *Journal of the American Academy of Child and Adolescent Psychiatry, 34*(4), 454–463.

Lewinsohn, P. M., Klein, D. N., & Seeley, J. R. (2000). Bipolar disorder during adolescence and young adulthood in a community sample. *Bipolar Disorder, 2,* 281–293.

Liebenluft, E., Charney, D. S., Towbin, K. E., Bhangoo, R. K., & Pine, D. S. (2003). Defining clinical phenotypes of juvenile mania. *American Journal of Psychiatry, 160,* 430–437.

Loebel, A. D., Lieberman, J. A., Alvir, J. M. J., Mayerhoff, D. I., Geisler, S. H., & Szymanski, S. R. (1992). Duration of psychosis and outcome in first episode schizophrenia. *American Journal of Psychiatry, 149,* 1183–1188.

Luby, E. D., Marrazzi, M. A., & Kinzie, J. (1987). Letter to the editor. *Journal of Clinical Psychopharmacology, 7,* 52–53.

Luby, J. L., Heffelfinger, A. K., Mrakosky, C., Hessler, M. J., Brown, K. M., & Hildebrand, T. (2002). Preschool major depressive disorder: Preliminary validation for developmentally modified *DSM-IV* criteria. *Journal of the American Academy of Child and Adolescent Psychiatry, 41*(8), 928–937.

Mahler, J. (2004, November 21). The antidepressant dilemma. *New York Times,* Section 6, p. 59.

Manji, H. K. (2001). The neurobiology of bipolar disorder. *Economics of Neuroscience, 3,* 37–44.

Manji, H. K., Moore, G. J., Rajowska, G., & Chen, G. (2000). Neuroplasticity and cellular resilience in mood disorders. *Molecular Psychiatry, 5,* 578–593.

Mannuzza, S., Klein, R. G., & Moulton, J. L. (2003). Does stimulant treatment place children at risk for adult substance abuse? A controlled, prospective follow-up study. *Journal of Child and Adolescent Psychopharmacology, 13*(3), 273–282.

March, J. S., Franklin, M., Nelson, A., & Foa, E. (2001). Cognitive-behavioral psychotherapy for pediatric obsessive-compulsive disorder. *Journal of Clinical Child Psychology, 30,* 8–18.

March, J., Silva, J., Petrycki, S., Curry, J., Wells, K., Fairbank, J., et al. (2004). Fluoxetine, cognitive-behavioral therapy and their combination for adolescents with depression. *Journal of the American Medical Association, 292,* 807–820.

Masi G., Perugi, G., Toni, C., Millepiedi, S., Mucci, M., Bertini, N., & Akiskal, H. S. (2004). Obsessive-compulsive bipolar comorbidity: focus on children and adolescents. *Journal of Affective Disorders, 78*(3), 175–183.

McDougle, C. J., Holmes, J. P., Carlson, D. C., Pelton, G. H., & Price, L. H. (1998). A double-blind, placebo-controlled study of risperidone in adults with autistic disorder and other pervasive developmental disorders. *Archives of General Psychiatry, 55*(7), 633–641.

MTA Cooperative Group. (1999). A 14-month randomized clinical trial of treatment strategies for ADHD. *Archives of General Psychiatry, 56*(12), 1073–1086.

National Center on Addiction and Substance Abuse. (2004). Report. Retrieved from www.casacolumbia.org.

Nobile, M., Cataldo, G. M., Marino, C., & Molteni, M. (2003). Diagnosis and treatment of dysthymia in children and adolescents. *CNS Drugs, 17*(13), 927–946.

Nurnberger, J. I., & Foroud, T. (2000). Genetics of bipolar affective disorder. *Current Psychiatry Reports, 2,* 147–157.

Papolos, D., & Papolos, J. (2007). *The bipolar child.* New York: Broadway Books.

Pediatric OCD Treatment Study (POTS) Team. (2004). Cognitive-behavior therapy, sertraline and their combination for children and adolescents with obsessive-compulsive disorder. *Journal of the American Medical Association, 292*(16), 1969–1976.

Pliszka, S., Greenhill, L. L., Crismon, M. L., Sedillo, A., Carlson, C., Conners, C. K., et al. (2000). The Texas Children's Medication Algorithm Project: Report of the Texas Consensus Conference panel on medication treatment of childhood attention deficit/hyperactivity disorder. *Journal of the American Academy of Child and Adolescent Psychiatry, 39*(7), 908–927.

Popper, C. (2004). Bipolar disorder in children and adolescents. *Audio Digest Psychiatry, 33*(2).

Potash, J. B., & DePaulo, J. R. (2000). Searching high and low: A review of the genetics of bipolar disorder. *Bipolar Disorder, 2,* 8–26.

Purdon, S. E., Wilson, L., Labelle, A., & Jones, B. D. (1994). Risperidone in the treatment of pervasive developmental disorder. *Canadian Journal of Psychiatry, 39,* 400–405.

Research Unit on Pediatric Psychopharmacology Anxiety Study Group. (2001). Fluvoxamine for the treatment of anxiety disorders in children and adolescents. *New England Journal of Medicine, 344,* 1279–1285.

Rett, A. (1977). Uber ein zerebral-atrophisches Syndrom bei Hyperammoniamie. [A cerebral atrophy associated with hyperam-monaemia.] In P. J. Vinken & G. W. Bruyn (Eds.), *Handbook of Clinical Neurology.* Amsterdam, North-Holland. (Original work published 1966).

Robertson, M. M., & Stern, J. S. (1997). The Gilles de la Tourette syndrome. *Critical Reviews in Neurobiology, 11,* 1–19.

Rosenberg, D. R., Mirza, Y., Russell, A., Tang, J., Smith, J. M., Banerjee, S. P., et al. (2004). Reduced anterior cingulate glutamatergic concentrations in childhood OCD and major depression versus healthy controls. *Journal of the American Academy of Child and Adolescent Psychiatry, 43,* 1146–1153.

Russell, A., Cortese, B., Lorch, E., Ivey, J., Banerjee, S. P., Moore, G. J., et al. (2003). Localized functional neurochemical marker abnormalities in dorsolateral prefrontal cortex in pediatric obsessive-compulsive disorder. *Journal of Child and Adolescent Psychopharmacology, 13*(Suppl. 1), S31–38.

Sachs, G. S., Baldassano, C. F., Truman, C. J., & Guille, C. (2000). Comorbidity of attention deficit hyperactivity disorder with early- and late-onset bipolar disorder. *American Journal of Psychiatry, 157,* 466–468.

Safer, D. J., & Krager, J. M. (1992). Effect of a media blitz and a threatened lawsuit on stimulant treatment. *Journal of the American Medical Association, 268,* 1004–1007.

Saxena, S., Brody, A. L., Ho, M. L., Zohrabi, N., Maidment, K. M., & Baxter, L. R., Jr. (2003). Differential brain metabolic predictors of response to paroxetine in obsessive-compulsive disorder versus major depression. *American Journal of Psychiatry, 160,* 522–532.

Schwartz, C. E., Snidman, N., & Kagan, J. (1999). Adolescent social anxiety as an outcome of inhibited temperament in childhood. *Journal of the American Academy of Child and Adolescent Psychiatry, 38,* 1008–1015.

Silverstone, P. H., Asghar, S. J., O'Donnell, T., Ulrich, M., & Hanstock, C. C. (2004). Lithium and valproate protect against dextro-amphetamine induced brain choline concentration changes in bipolar disorder patients. *World Journal of Biological Psychiatry, 5*(1), 38–44.

Soares, J. C., & Mann, J. J. (1997). The anatomy of mood disorders: Review of structural neuroimaging studies. *Biological Psychiatry, 41,* 86–106.

Snider, L. A., & Swedo, S. E. (2004). PANDAS: Current status and directions for research. *Molecular Psychiatry, 10,* 900–907.

Stern, E., Silbersweig, D. A., Chee, K., Holmes, A., Robertson, M. M., Trimble, M., et al. (2000). A functional neuroanatomy of tics in Tourette syndrome. *Archives of General Psychiatry, 57,* 741–748.

STEP-BD Program (Systematic Treatment Enhancement Program for Bipolar Disorder: National Institute of Mental Health). (2008). www.nimh.gov/health/trials/practical/step-bd/index.shtml/.

Thomsen, P. H., Ebbesen, C., & Persson, C. (2001). Long-term experience with citalopram in the treatment of adolescent OCD. *Journal of the American Academy of Child and Adolescent Psychiatry, 40,* 895–902.

Tolin, D. F., Abramowitz, J. S., Kozak, M. J., & Foa, E. B. (2001). Fixity of belief, perceptual aberration, and magical ideation in obsessive-compulsive disorder. *Journal of Anxiety Disorders, 15,* 501–10.

Tsai, L. Y. (2004). Autistic disorder and other pervasive developmental disorders. In J. M. Wiener & M. K. Dulcan (Eds.), *The APA textbook of child and adolescent psychiatry* (pp. 261–349). Arlington, VA: American Psychiatric Publishing, Inc.

Tsuang, M. T., & Faraone, S. V. 1990. *The Genetics of Mood Disorders.* Baltimore: Johns Hopkins University Press.

Wagner, K. D., Ambrosini, P., Ryann, M., Wohlberg, C., Yang, R., Greenbaum, M.S., et al. (2003). Efficacy of sertraline in the treatment of children and adolescents with major depression disorder: Two randomized, controlled trials. *Journal of the American Medical Association, 290,* 1033–1041.

Walkup, J. (2004). Child and adolescent psychopharmacology: What's new? Paper presented at the U.S. Psychiatric and Mental Health Congress in November 18, San Diego, CA.

Weng, G., Bhalla, U.S., & Iyengar, R. (1999). Complexity in biological signaling systems. *Science, 284,* 92–96.

Whittington, C. J., Kendall, T., Fonagy, P., Cottrell, D., Cotgrove, A., & Boddington, E. (2004). SSRIs in childhood depression: Systematic review of published versus unpublished data. *Lancet, 363*(9418), 1341–1345.

Wozniak, J., Biederman, J., Mounteaux, M. C., Richards, J., & Faraone, S. V. (2002). Parsing the comorbidity between bipolar disorder and anxiety disorders: A familial risk analysis. *Journal of Child and Adolescent Psychopharmacology, 12*(2), 101–111.

Wozniak, J., Biederman, J., Mundy, E., Mennin, D, & Faraone, S. V. (1995). A pilot family study of childhood-onset mania. *Journal of the American Academy of Child and Adolescent Psychiatry, 34,* 1577–1583.

John D. Preston, Psy.D., ABPP, is professor emeritus at Alliant International University in Sacramento, CA, and has also served on the faculty of the University of California, Davis, School of Medicine and the Professional School of Psychology, San Francisco. He has authored twenty books in the areas of psychotherapy, neurobiology, and psychopharmacology, and coauthored *Clinical Psychopharmacology Made Ridiculously Simple* and *Handbook of Clinical Psychopharmacology for Therapists*. Preston is a fellow of the American Psychological Association and has lectured internationally.

John H. O'Neal, MD, is a board-certified psychiatrist at Kaiser Sacramento Medical Center and assistant clinical professor in the department of psychiatry at the University of California, Davis, School of Medicine. He was in private practice for over twenty years and is past chief of the Department of Psychiatry at Sutter Community Hospitals in Sacramento, CA. O'Neal is a fellow of the American Psychological Association and lectures on depression and psychopharmacology to mental health professionals, self-help organizations, and the public. He is coauthor of *Handbook of Clinical Psychopharmacology for Therapists*.

Mary C. Talaga, R.Ph., Ph.D., is administrative services leader for Kaiser Permanente Pharmacy Operations, Northern California Region. She has been a pharmacist for over thirty years, with specialization in psychiatric pharmacy. Talaga has practiced in a variety of clinical settings and provides training and mentoring to health care professionals as well as general education to patients and consumers. She is coauthor of *Handbook of Clinical Psychopharmacology for Therapists*.

John Preston, John O'Neal, and Mary Talaga are coauthors of *The Handbook of Clinical Psychopharmacology for Therapists*, now in its sixth edition.

Index

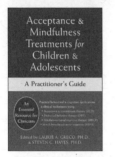

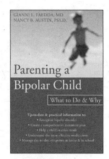